NOSTRADAMUS

THE FINAL RECKONING

By the same author

THE ARMAGEDDON SCRIPT

BEYOND ALL BELIEF

THE COSMIC EYE

GOSPEL OF THE STARS

THE GREAT PYRAMID DECODED

THE GREAT PYRAMID: YOUR PERSONAL GUIDE

THE HEALING OF THE GODS

THIS NEW AGE BUSINESS

NOSTRADAMUS—THE NEXT 50 YEARS

NOSTRADAMUS

THE FINAL RECKONING

Peter Lemesurier

BERKLEY BOOKS, NEW YORK

Most of the verse translations of Nostradamus quoted in this book are originals. The rest are taken (sometimes in marginally improved versions) from *Nostradamus—The Next 50 Years* by Peter Lemesurier (Piatkus 1993). This latter is the first (and, to date, the only) English verse translation of the prophecies. Arranged into a convincing, more or less continuous, sequence of future events, it is recommended as a textual companion to this volume.

NOSTRADAMUS: THE FINAL RECKONING

A Berkley Book / published by arrangement with
Piatkus Books

PRINTING HISTORY
Piatkus edition published 1995
Berkley trade paperback edition / January 1997

Book design by Maureen Troy.
Sketch maps by the author.
Artwork on page 106 is reproduced by permission of Element Books.

For information address: Judy Piatkus (Publishers) Ltd,
5 Windmill Street, London W1P 1HF.

The Putnam Berkley World Wide Web site address is
http://www.berkley.com/berkley

ISBN: 0-425-15610-9

BERKLEY®
Berkley Books are published by The Berkley Publishing Group,
200 Madison Avenue, New York, New York 10016.
BERKLEY and the "B" design
are trademarks belonging to Berkley Publishing Corporation.

PRINTED IN THE UNITED STATES OF AMERICA

10 9 8 7 6 5 4 3 2 1

Contents

Superscript numerals in the text refer to the numbered publications in the Reference–Bibliography at the end of the book.

Introduction:
Appointment With Destiny

EVERYBODY, SURELY, HAS HEARD OF NOSTRADAMUS AND HIS CELebrated thousand-odd prophecies. Everybody must by now be aware that they are supposed to reveal what is destined to happen to our world for centuries to come. But the big question that nobody has so far managed to answer satisfactorily is '*When*?'

This is a real problem.

If my dentist promises to fix my teeth, after all, that promise is worse than useless unless she also says when. If there is no date, then there is no appointment.

Much the same applies to those larger appointments with destiny that are the world's great prophecies. They may quite safely promise us war or peace, famine or plenty, doom or triumph, misery or joy—for assuredly the future will bring us plenty of each—but unless they also say *when*, they are not true prophecies at all.

The bookshops are full of books containing such undated predictions and, people being only human, thousands every day buy them, read them, and imagine that they are being told something new. In reality they are merely being told a very old story indeed.

This book, by contrast, is positively stuffed with dates. In fact there are over 150 of them. In what is a major breakthrough where Nostradamus's prophecies are concerned, it finally succeeds in answering the question 'When?' Moreover, it does so by perfectly reasonable and scientific means that owe nothing to superstition or wishful thinking. It also supplements the Nostradamian revelations with dated predictions from other major prophets, too, and discovers a remarkably explicit general consensus among them.

The upshot is a stunning one. The over-all sequence of major future events, it transpires, has already been mapped out from 1995 until at least the year 4000.

And that—after a brief survey of the various prophetic sources—is what this book duly presents.

The account, inevitably, is dramatic, but not *melo*dramatic. It does not indulge in vague, credulous speculation. Brutal it may sometimes be—for so is reality itself—but it spares you the usual sensationalist scenarios of virtually unmitigated universal doom. It imposes no preconceived agendas. Thoughtful though it is, it does not fantasize beyond the matter in hand. It does not need to. The major prophets are perfectly clear and very nearly unanimous in what they have to say.

The major seismic events of the near future, the accession and coronation of a new King of England, the decidedly gloomy future of the Popes, the coming Islamic invasion and virtual destruction of southern and western Europe, the siege and bombardment of Britain, the long-delayed Western counter-attack, the ensuing age of peace and plenty, the era of renewed cataclysm and decline, the eventual extraterrestrial Saviours, the era of interplanetary travel, the ultimate transformation of humanity—all are spelt out citing exact chapter and verse (at least where Nostradamus is concerned) so that you, the reader, can refer to his prophecies and measure them against actual events as they develop.

And the book's closing pages will help you to assess how likely they are and what, if anything, all this really means for us.

As a long-time writer on prophecy and related subjects, as

well as the author of the first sequenced verse-translation of Nostradamus into English, I am sometimes asked if I believe such prophecies. I invariably answer, 'No.' Indeed, I cannot even begin to imagine how the prophetic faculty might work in the first place. Ultimately, though, it is not a matter of belief or of theory, but of simple observation. Either the predictions will come true, or they will not. And in the light of today's developing world-situation, I have to say that the major events mooted in this book seem to me to be not only more and more likely, but drawing ever closer.

But then I could, of course, be wrong.

You, similarly, may believe or disbelieve what this book has to say. Nobody is asking you to undertake any act of faith. The infallibility of Nostradamus and the other seers is not at issue. You are merely invited to read, then wait and see.

And if the prophecies start turning out to be right, you may well then feel inclined to think with me about the deeper lessons that they also carry with them. For that was ever the prime purpose of prophecy.

In short, the time may then have come to act.

NOSTRADAMUS

THE FINAL RECKONING

Part One

Probing the Future

1

The Unknown Tomorrow

THIS IS MORE THAN JUST A BOOK ABOUT THE FUTURE. IT IS A *history* of the future. This may seem a surprising claim to make. Yet it is true in at least two important respects. Not only has the broad outline of that future already been written, quite literally, by seers and prophets throughout the ages but, more importantly, it has also already been written in the much deeper sense that we human beings—all of us—have ourselves largely contrived to write it.

And we have done so through our own past thoughts and actions.

The future, in other words, is not inflicted on us by some malign fate, or by malevolent beings or influences 'out there'. It is essentially a do-it-yourself job. If it looks messy, then this is because we ourselves have already made a mess of it. And if we want it to look less messy, it is we alone who can do something about it.

The future, then, concerns us all—in both senses of the word. Indeed, it does far more than merely concern us. It enthrals us, fascinates us, terrifies us. So deeply are most of us in thrall to it that we gear much of our childhood, most of our education, even more of our working life and virtually the whole of our spiritual life to its supposed demands. What sort of person will I become? What job will I get? How large will my pension be? Shall I survive long enough to collect it? Will there be anybody to pay it even if I do? And what will happen to me when I die?

Fear of the unknown

This life-long obsession with the future is fundamentally rooted in insecurity. It is there precisely because we do not know what is coming. Aside from the workings of our inner unconscious, it represents the great unknown in our life. To a large extent it could be described as our 'outer unconscious'. And ignorance was ever the mother of fear.

We know, after all, that the universe has successfully brought us thus far (astonishing though that may sometimes seem in hindsight). We know that we are here now (surprising though that, too, may sometimes seem). But always the great unknown rears its worrying head in the form of the questions: 'Shall we be here tomorrow? And if so, what joys and sorrows, what pains and terrors will that tomorrow bring?'

Not that answering such questions necessarily helps very much. The answers that we are given may not be reliable—a possibility that merely spells even more insecurity for us. Besides, if the future holds joys for us, we still want to know how long they will last; if terrors, whether we shall be able to survive them. Even the certainty of death somehow manages to fill us with uncertainty, for we still cannot be sure when it will come, how it will feel or what, if anything, lies beyond it.

Our search for the future

And so it is no wonder that we constantly feel the need to peer anxiously into the future. The results are obvious for all to see. We watch the weather-forecast as though our lives depended on it (even when they don't); we read the opinion polls and treat them as though they were predictions (even though they aren't); we listen to the economic pundits and political spin-doctors as though they know what they are talking about (even when they don't); we read our horoscopes or consult the

Tarot as though they were reliable (even if they have been wrong before). Even our alleged 'news' programmes tend increasingly to be at least as much about what is about to happen as about what already has.

But all this is of course pretty small beer by comparison with the larger picture. When it comes to answering big questions such as what is going to happen to the world as a whole in five or ten years' time, or even half-a-century hence, we are even more keen to find out what is likely to happen. For it will inevitably affect not merely our own future, but that of our children and grandchildren too—and, in the face of such mighty events, we as individuals naturally feel even more threatened and powerless than ever (oblivious of the fact that, if we human beings have largely caused those events, then we are perfectly capable of *un*causing them too). Yet, paradoxically, it is in this very sphere that we are even less likely to get reliable answers from our forecasters, planners, pundits, politicians, and astrologers.

The seers

Fortunately, it is here that the world's great seers and sages come to our rescue. Or at least they claim to. The problem, though, is the self-same one as before. We just cannot be sure, even about *them*. Just how accurate, after all, are they really likely to be? How can we know that they speak the truth? And how (to be quite rational, scientific and down-to-earth about it) could anybody possibly manage to foretell the future anyway?

Indeed, is such an undertaking really likely to be such a good idea in the first place, even if it is possible? Might it not be tantamount to interfering in God's private business? How much are we mere mortals really meant to know about such things? And might not dabbling in the occult—for that, by definition, is what it amounts to, since 'the occult' simply means 'the hidden'—bring down upon our heads the very disasters that we most wish to avoid?

Indeed, might it not lead to something even more terrifying?

Might it not force us at last to face up to the dreaded consequences—hitherto, perhaps, either unknown or blithely disregarded—of our own past and present acts? Might it not even throw into question our very way of life and the assumptions and traditional systems of thought on which it is based?

Assessing the sources

Certainly such questions need to be addressed, for if knowledge of the future is as important to us as it certainly seems to be, then we need to be sure of our sources and confident in what we are about. And since nobody to date has managed to come up with a theory of precognition that commands much general agreement, there is only one thing for it: we have to rely almost exclusively on the various seers' proven track-records. As with many medical cures, in other words, we may not know exactly *how* it is done, but at least we need to make sure *that* it *has* been done—and to positive and unthreatening effect, at that. Which in turn means that, if we are to open any kind of reliable window on our future, then we should be wise to look at sources that have been around for some years now, rather than ones—however impressive, brilliant, modern or computerised—that have only recently arrived on the scene.

Thus, though we may consult a whole range of sources ranging from the ancient scriptures of both East and West to the acknowledged prophets of medieval times, it is only the more venerable of our modern seers who are likely to merit our attention here. In particular, we shall need to focus on prophets who are actually prepared to tell us *when*—whether by giving us specific dates, by arranging their predictions in sequence or by tying them in with other events such as astronomical cycles, geophysical phenomena or even other prophecies.

For otherwise, their prophecies are scarcely prophecies at all.

Nevertheless, this still leaves us a large field to choose from, and one in which the various track-records are by now well-enough known for us to make a reasonable selection. Set out in the next chapter, consequently, are details of the more important sources that I shall be using in this book to establish an overview of the world's likely future.

2

The Sources

THE FOLLOWING IS A BRIEF SURVEY OF THE MAIN PROPHETIC sources that I shall be using to construct the calendar of future events offered in Parts 2 and 3. They are arranged in more or less chronological order.

The Great Pyramid

By far the most ancient of the sources directly available to us, the Great Pyramid of Giza in Egypt was built (according to most authorities) at least 2,600 years before the birth of Christ. Its proposed functions have latterly ranged from a tomb, via a cenotaph, a treasure-house, an agricultural store, an astronomical observatory, a weights-and-measures standard, a theodolite, a cosmic power-house, an Atlantean time-capsule, an irrigation pump for the Nile delta and a scientific databank, to a massive meditation aid and temple of initiation. On statistical grounds alone, most of these descriptions would no doubt have surprised its original designers more than a little—whoever they may have been.

Quite apart from all this, however, it has long been recognised that its passages and chambers look—for whatever reason—uncannily like a blueprint for human history, expressed in terms of the various passages' angles, directions, sizes and shapes, as well as through the types of stone used. Indeed, the celebrated psychic **Edgar Cayce** (one of our subsequent sources) himself affirmed as much. There even seems to be some sort of timescale in operation—one so precise, in fact, as to pinpoint not only the years, but in some cases the *exact days* when a number of major past events have occurred. The passageways, in other words, may indeed represent the post-mortem path of the Osirian soul, but they also represent the historical path of the living soul of humanity itself.

Refer to the following diagram, for example, and you will see that the so-called 'Scored Lines' (a little way down in from the entrance to the passageways, on the right of the diagram) are shown as marking a date of 2141 BC: this is because it was in that year alone (at noon on 21 March, to be precise) that these deliberately incised marks in either wall of the passage pointed at Alcyone, chief star of the Pleiades (part of the then-'ruling' constellation of Taurus—see the next section, below, on aeonic astrology) while the passage itself was aligned with Alpha Draconis, the then Pole Star, at its lower culmination (and thus with True North). Evidently, then (the argument goes), this represents the astronomical datum for the whole passage-system and the 'Go' mark for the ensuing game of cosmic Snakes-and-Ladders that is humanity's life here on this planet.

However, for this system to 'work', there also has to be some kind of dating-system or timescale. As it happens, there is. Initially, at least, this seems to be one year for every so-called Primitive Inch (equal to 1.00106 British inches or 2.54268 cm) from north to south along the sloping passage-floors.

Thus, measuring back from the Scored Lines to the designed entrance on this same scale brings us to the summer solstice of the year 2623 BC—which is not only astronomically impressive, but also falls squarely within the presumed dates of King Khufu, or Cheops, who is supposed to have built the monument in the first place. Clearly, then, the 'timescale' theory is a promising one.

This immediately suggests that we should now measure *forwards* on the same basis. Doing so brings us to the beginning of the Ascending Passage—obviously some kind of 'parting of the ways'—in the spring of 1453 BC, which some scholars insist

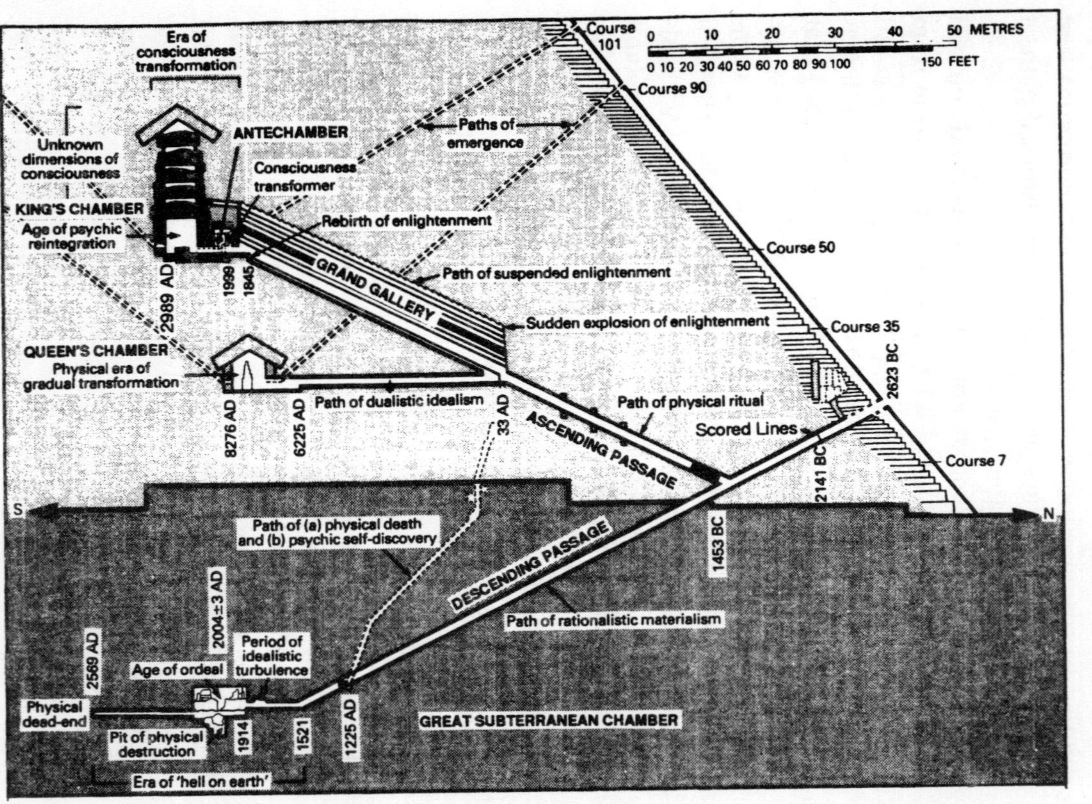

At-a-glance summary chart of the Pyramid's prophetic blueprint for humanity

was the very year of the celebrated Israelite Exodus from Egypt: and not just on any old date, either, *but on 30 March*, which for astronomical reasons has to be the actual date of that first Passover, if 1453 BC was indeed the year in question.

If, suitably encouraged, we now measure our way up the Ascending Passage in the same way, we find that we arrive at a sudden rise in roof-level (i.e. symbolically a 'raising of the roof') at the beginning of the Pyramid's astonishing Grand Gallery on 1 April, AD 33—which naturally begs identification (however improbable this particular outcome may seem) as the date of the Crucifixion. And if, continuing onwards and up the slope, we go on to discover that the roof finally 'comes back down to earth again' at the summer solstice of the fateful year 1914—a mere week before the assassination in Sarajevo of the Austrian Archduke Ferdinand that precipitated the subsequent outbreak of the First World War—this further fact starts, after all, not to seem so very surprising.

The Descending Passage, meanwhile, has finally 'hit rock bottom' between the years 1440 and 1521, so apparently marking the very much 'back to basics' aspect of the Renaissance and everything that flowed from it not merely in Europe, but all over the world. Following a carefully carved 'roof fall'—i.e. an evidently turbulent period during which 'the roof falls in'—between 1767 and 1848 (the latter being known to this day as 'the Year of Revolutions') the resulting Subterranean Passage finally tumbles into the 'Chamber of Ordeal' in (once again) the summer of 1914.

It follows, then, that the ghastly Great Subterranean Chamber, with its treacherous, uneven floor, the abrupt ups and downs of its transverse rock ridges and its symbolic 'bottomless pit', must in some way represent our own times. And indeed, it appears to do just that. The 'depressed periods' of the First World War, of the 1930s and of the succeeding Second World War seem to be well indicated, as does the revival of the 1950s and 1960s. Subsequent downturns seem to correspond well to the sudden uncertainties of the late 1960s onwards as represented by the 1973/4 oil crisis, the subsequent economic slump and the world trade-recessions of the early 1980s and 1990s. And ahead of us still lies the yawning pit . . .

But if the Great Subterranean Chamber maps out the ups and downs of our present age and of the years directly ahead of us, so equally must the apparent heavenly initiatives and ultimate 'open tomb' that ensue in the upper passageways. And this is to say nothing of the 'alternative destiny' apparently mapped out by the somewhat lower (and thus 'inferior') Queen's Chamber and its passage, let alone the further dimensions of existence evidently promised by the five 'secret chambers' that tower up into the darkness above the final King's Chamber.

It all seems too neat and coincidental to be true, of course. But with so many 'coincidences' (and these are by no means the end of them where the Great Pyramid is concerned) one has to start suspecting that they may, after all, not be coincidences at all, and that we may have in the Great Pyramid a powerful predictive tool (designed by who knows whom) for reading our likely future.

For well over a century now, consequently, efforts have been made to do precisely that. In 1977 I was able, by building on the considerable decoding efforts of various predecessors—notably Davidson, the Edgar brothers and Adam Rutherford—to publish an even more sophisticated analysis entitled *The Great Pyramid Decoded* (Element, 1977) which, however imperfect, is widely acknowledged to be the most advanced currently available. To date, the history of recent events seems broadly to have fitted the conclusions I arrived at, if sometimes in surprising ways, and it is consequently to that analysis—and its sequel in *The Great Pyramid: Your Personal Guide* (Element, 1987)—that I shall be referring in the following pages.

Aeonic astrology

Aeonic astrology is the astrology of the succeeding zodiacal 'ages' through which our planet is said to pass in the course of its 2,600-year precessional cycle. It is based on the observation that, once every 2,000 years or so, the sun's position at the spring equinox appears to move 'backwards' into a different sign of the zodiac—which means, of course, that it will eventually return to the point where it 'started', only to begin the cycle all over again. Thus, the system, in the nature of things, is unlikely to have been devised much before 2000 BC, when it was first noticed that the position of the full moon nearest the autumn equinox (the original celestial marker) was unaccountably moving out of its home-sign of Taurus and into Aries—which, in terms of known dates and astrological antecedents, would argue for an ancient Babylonian origin.

With the advent of solar astrology during classical times the system was refined and regulated to the point where it is now possible to assign fairly firm dates to the transition from sign to sign, and consequently from age to age. Various of the classical gods—later assimilated to the planets—were also allocated to the various signs. This made it possible not merely to date the successive ages, but actually to pinpoint their likely natures.

Thus, to take a few past examples, the period between roughly the dates 4000 and 2000 BC was historically the age of Taurus, the Bull. Perhaps it is no accident, then, that this was the age during which the precursors of the great bull-cults of the Middle East first arose—whether of the Semitic El, of the Winged Bull of Nineveh, of the Greek Zeus and Poseidon, of the Cretan Minotaur, of the Persian Mithras, of the Egyptian Apis or of the biblical Golden Calf against which the later Moses was to rail so furiously. And if the ancient Phoenician alphabet to whose successors we ourselves are heirs also began at about that time with the sign of the Bull (𐤀, the precursor of the Greek *alpha*), perhaps this was only to be expected.

The age that followed (roughly 2000 BC to the dawn of Christianity) was that of Aries, the Ram, which was said to be ruled by Mars, the warlike leader. And so, once again, the earthly cults started to reflect the fact, as did the characteristic attitudes of the time. The predominant Egyptian cult became that of Amun, the Ram-god, while the Israelites were forced by the angry Moses to abandon their bull-cult for that of the Passover Lamb. Meanwhile discipline and conformity became all, as the great Arian high priests and initiates—Ikhnaton, Zoroaster, Lao Tzu, Confucius, the Buddha, Pythagoras, Plato and Aristotle among them—shepherded their reluctant flocks towards their future destiny.

And so it was that the age of Pisces arrived—evidently an age for a growing measure of freedom and even slipperiness, if not for a whole new dimension of existence—and with it Jesus of Nazareth, who deliberately chose his disciples largely from among fishermen and constantly demonstrated his teachings to them in terms of catches of fish, multiplications of fish, meals of fish. It is no surprise, then, that his subsequent followers should have referred to themselves as 'fishes', taken the fish as their secret sign, instituted a ceremony representing drowning-and-rebirth as their rite of entry and referred to their leaders by the Greek term *episkopos*, which actually contains the Latin root for 'fish' (*pisc-*). And if the resulting 'bishop' then chose to haul his catch into the *nave* that was the 'ship' of the church, while leaning on the shepherd's crook of Aries and wearing on his head a hat in the shape of a fish with an open mouth . . . that was all sheer bonus.

We today are still living in that self-same age of Pisces. The coming 'Age of Aquarius' is due to succeed it sometime during the first half of the coming millennium (though certainly no earlier than the year 2010). Almost the only book to set out this system in full and to explore the likely implications for us is my own *Gospel of the Stars* (Element, 1977), and it is therefore in terms of this that I shall be arguing in the following pages.

The Hindu and Buddhist scriptures

Like most of the world's sacred writings, neither the Hindu nor the Buddhist scriptures attempt to set out very much in the way of dates for specific future events. Nevertheless, they do contain a clear cosmology which in turn presupposes a fixed prophetic timescale.

The figures, as set out in books such as the *Vishnu Purana*, are well enough known.[14] The universe, it is claimed, is subject to an over-all 'day-night' cycle of existence and non-existence—a kind of oscillating-universe cycle—lasting some 8,640 million years. The 'day' or 'manifest' half of this cycle is made up of a thousand *Mahayugas*, or Great Ages, each in turn comprising four succeeding ages of mounting corruption and depravity whose respective lengths stand to each other in the proportions 4:3:2:1.

This means, in effect, that the human race is supposed to have been in a state of primal bliss from around four million years ago until some two million years ago (the era known as the *Satya Yuga* or *Krita Yuga*). Following this 'Golden Age', a long and gradual decline in human nobility, piety and morals started to set in (the *Treta Yuga*), leading to the onset some 870,000 years ago of a much steeper decline during the ensuing *Dvapara Yuga*.

The shortest and nastiest of the four ages is thus the last, the *Kali Yuga*—and this turns out to be our own, which started in the year 3102 BC and is destined to last all of 432,000 years. During it religion and spirituality will be progressively abandoned, and the earth will be swept by fire, drought and famine. For a hundred years world-wide death and destruction will ensue, after which a further massive drought will usher in the final planetary holocaust at the hands of the future avatar of Vishnu known as Kalki, a horse-headed giant who will wield a fiery sword like a comet. Following this, not only the universe itself, but its Creator too, will cease to exist for a further period of 4,320 million years—the so-called 'Night of Brahma'—and it is only in the new universe which will then be reborn that there is any prospect of a new Golden Age.

This scheme of things was, naturally enough, taken over more or less lock, stock and barrel by Hinduism's spiritual successor, Buddhism, if with a different cast of characters—which means that Maitreya, the Buddhists' much milder counterpart of Vishnu-as-Kalki, is similarly unlikely to appear to set the universe to rights until some half-a-million years hence, despite the well-meaning insistence of New Age activists such as Benjamin Creme that he is already alive and well and living in the East End of London.[14]

Rather more interesting and relevant, possibly, is the fact that the original Hindu numbers correspond remarkably closely to the datings nowadays proposed by palaeontologists such as Richard Leakey for the various parallel developments in the evolution of humanity.[14] The period of the *Satya Yuga*, or Golden Age, would seem more or less to match that of the early, pre-linguistic types of hominid who, lacking language, would presumably have been living in a blissful, quasi-animal state—or at least one in which such painful sentiments as guilt and regret were largely absent. The dates of the ensuing *Treta Yuga* mark the period during which changes in the shape of the human cranium were first starting to make language possible, and thus also, perhaps, some kind of 'fall from grace' rooted in the development of human consciousness. The period of the *Dvapara Yuga* comfortably encompasses the era during which the even more linguistically developed *homo sapiens* first put in his appearance. And the onset of the final age of the cycle—the so-called 'Age of Iron'—meshes in well with the beginning of the age of agriculture and settled communities, with all their opportunities for further moral and religious decline.

Probable or improbable, though, neither the Hindu nor the Buddhist scheme of things tells us very much about any future events that could possibly affect us directly (or at least, as the Hindus and the less logical of the Buddhists would put it, not in our present incarnations). On the other hand, they do paint for us a general backcloth which may at least help to lend context to our prophetic quest.

The Bible

To such an extent was prophecy a major concern of the Hebrew Bible—now better known to us as the Old Testament—

that at the time of Jesus it was actually divided into two sections known as 'The Law' and 'The Prophets'. Jesus himself actually referred to it as such. From Moses, through a whole succession of prophets from the eighth-century Isaiah to the fourth-century Joel—not forgetting the prophecies attributed to Daniel (part of a third, subsequent section known as 'The Writings') that were apparently faked as late as the second century BC—the whole history and fate of the Israelite nation was seen in terms of its success or failure in living up to a kind of prophetic blueprint allegedly laid down through the prophets by God himself.

The Old Testament prophecies, consequently, are many and complex, and by no means all of them are entirely free of the suspicion of having been written down after the event. Nevertheless, it has to be admitted that nearly all of them—from predictions of the Assyrian and Babylonian invasions, the exile and return from Babylon and the subsequent Greek oppression and desecration of the Jerusalem temple, right down to personal prophecies for particular groups and leaders—were fulfilled in ancient times, leaving still unfulfilled only those referring to the end of the age and the coming of an expected future Jewish Messiah or liberating Priest-King.

As with their Hindu and Buddhist equivalents, however, the biblical prophecies do not concern themselves much with actual dates. True, the book of Daniel is unusual in that it offers a number of highly vague and complicated numerical rigmaroles that *look like* dates. These seem to have been designed to convince the author's contemporaries in suitably mysterious terms that the predicted Last Times and the ensuing Kingdom of Heaven were actually at hand, if only they cared to grasp the opportunity. In this they were actually successful, and a major uprising ensued to liberate the country from the Greek forces that were then occupying it. They also sparked the subsequent Messianic movement that would eventually produce Jesus himself. However, the very vagueness and complication of these predictions makes it possible to 'stretch' and reinterpret them to fit modern times, too, and Christian propagandists have not been slow to exploit the fact—and then to reinterpret them yet again when their calculations have proved wrong.

For our own purposes, then, by far the best plan seems to be to rely on what purports to be Jesus' own summary of the as-yet unfulfilled predictions in the so-called 'Little Apocalypse' of Matthew 24 (echoed at Mark 13 and Luke 21), together with the ancient 'third day' tradition picked up on by the second letter of Peter (3:8). These, after all, at least offer some kind of time-reference. The former, in particular, was actually designed as a list of 'Signs of the Times'—i.e. a kind of checklist against which to measure the imminence of the end of the age and the long-promised coming of the Jewish Messiah into his final kingdom.

Broadly, the picture (based closely on Old Testament prophets such as Isaiah, Micah, Jeremiah, Ezekiel, Zechariah, and Joel, along with the more recently 'discovered' Daniel) is of a long period of 'wars and rumours of wars', of famines and earthquakes, false Messiahs and religious persecutions—all of it accompanied by widespread misery and deprivation, as well as by mass-movements of refugees. The end of this period of unprecedented woes is to be signalled by the disappearance of sun, moon and stars, and possibly even by a cometary collision with the earth. Only then, when he is least expected, will the predicted Messiah finally appear to restore the dispersed Jews to their ancient homeland and pronounce judgement on the earth's peoples. Whereupon the sick will be healed, the blind made to see, the deaf to hear and the lame to walk: even the dead will be restored to life.

Interestingly enough, the prophesied return to the homeland seems already to have been happening since at least 1947, while medical science has long since embarked on fulfilling the list of other miracles, too.

At this point, referring to the 'three-day' tradition originally promulgated by Moses himself, Peter's letter interprets each 'day' in terms of a thousand years—which theoretically ought to mean that the Messiah is due to appear during the third millennium after the crucifixion—i.e. at any time from about

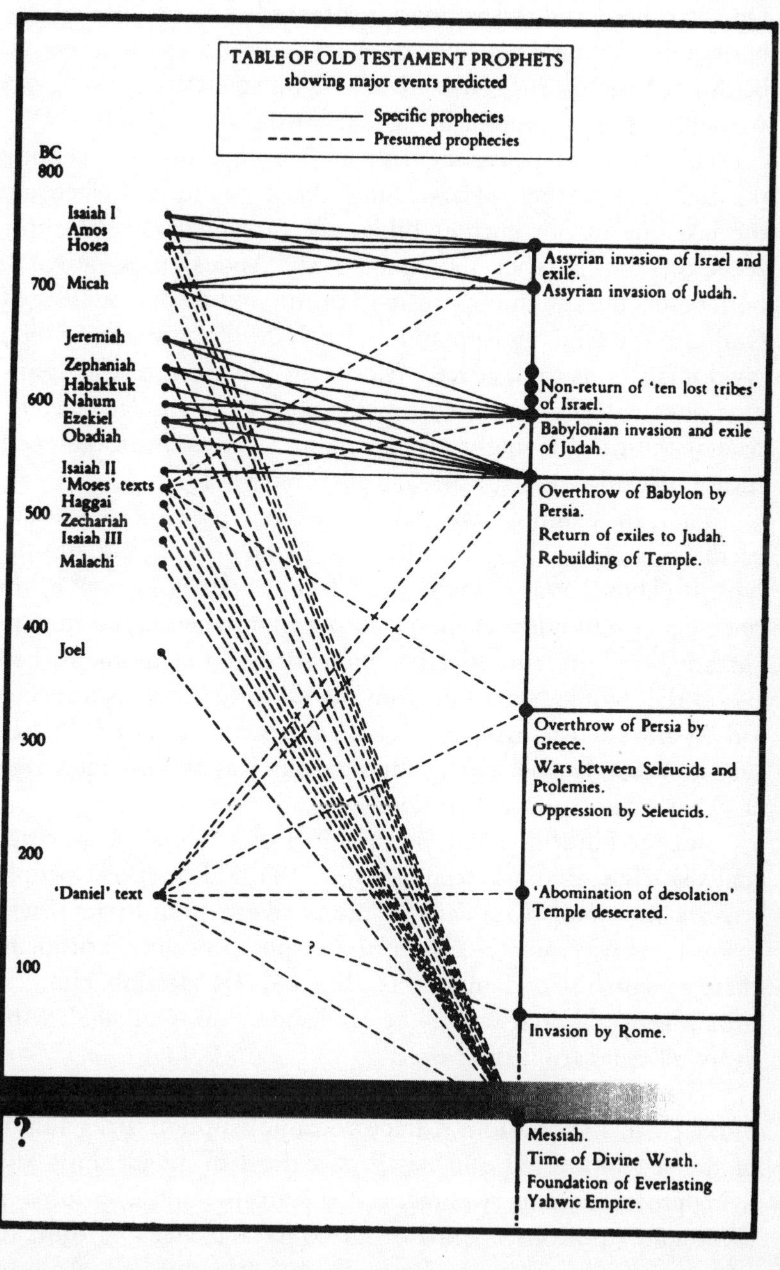
TABLE OF OLD TESTAMENT PROPHETS
showing major events predicted
Specific prophecies
Presumed prophecies
BC
800
Isaiah I
Amos
Hosea
700 Micah
Jeremiah
Zephaniah
Habakkuk
600 Nahum
Ezekiel
Obadiah
Isaiah II
'Moses' texts
Haggai
500 Zechariah
Isaiah III
Malachi
400
Joel
300
200
'Daniel' text
100
?
?
Assyrian invasion of Israel and exile.
Assyrian invasion of Judah.
Non-return of 'ten lost tribes' of Israel.
Babylonian invasion and exile of Judah.
Overthrow of Babylon by Persia.
Return of exiles to Judah.
Rebuilding of Temple.
Overthrow of Persia by Greece.
Wars between Seleucids and Ptolemies.
Oppression by Seleucids.
'Abomination of desolation' Temple desecrated.
Invasion by Rome.
Messiah.
Time of Divine Wrath.
Foundation of Everlasting Yahwic Empire.

the year 2033 onwards, and presumably no later than 3033. On the other hand, Jesus himself is recorded as saying that nobody, not even he, knew exactly when it would happen, though he did apparently suggest—mistakenly, if so—that it would occur within the lifetime of his listeners (Matthew 24:34).

This body of prophecy was in due course to be supplemented by a further, extraordinary book that was to become the last one in our current Bible—the so-called *Revelation of John*, one of a number of contemporary 'Apocalypses' designed both to encourage the oppressed faithful and to put the fear of God into the reigning Roman Empire. Indeed, this contains such vivid imagery as to have haunted the imaginations of Christians ever since with the distinct suspicion that, having failed to come true at the time, it might all happen at some point in our own future instead—perhaps as early as tomorrow.

To it, for example, we owe the celebrated vision of a future earth stalked by the dreaded Four Horsemen of the Apocalypse—Plague, War, Famine and Death respectively. We are once again reminded of the promised time when, amid mighty earthquakes, the sun will be dimmed and the moon turned blood-red. While 'stars fall from the sky', the heavens are convulsed and the earth is sent reeling, the earth's terrified peoples will desperately seek shelter underground as the dreaded Day of Wrath dawns (in Latin, *Dies Irae*).

But the faithful will be spared. In a direct echo of the original Israelite Exodus from Egypt, 144,000 marked people (twelve thousand from each of the twelve tribes of Israel) will make their way, white-clad, to the resplendent new Jerusalem, there to worship God and praise Him and His Messiah. Hunger, thirst, heat and cold will all be abolished, and 'God shall wipe away all tears from their eyes.'

There follows a rain of blood and fire that consumes a third of the earth's vegetation. A huge volcanic eruption turns a third of the sea blood-red and destroys a third of all its ships and living creatures. A fiery comet called Wormwood (*Chernobyl* in Ukrainian!) poisons a third of all rivers and wells. A third of sun, moon and stars are (once again!) extinguished. And an ominous eagle is seen flying in mid-heaven screeching 'Oee, oee, oee [Alas! Alas! Alas!] for the peoples of earth.'

Now comes another meteor or comet (or perhaps it is really the same one). This produces not only further violent volcanic eruptions but, issuing out of the resulting smoke, a huge swarm of locusts spreading across the earth. Their mission is to torment the ungodly to the point where they actually long to die. Wings whirring, but otherwise arrayed and equipped like Roman cavalry, they form a countless host more mighty than any seen before or since whose advance (preceded and followed by fire) turns every paradise into a wilderness, and the dust of whose thundering hooves obliterates (yet again!) the very sun, moon and stars.

And they are commanded by a Dark Angel from Hell, a veritable King of the Abyss called Abaddon ('Destroyer')—or, in Greek, Apollyon.

And so it all goes on until the Last Trumpet sounds, humanity is finally judged, the faithful are admitted to Paradise and the wicked are finally consigned to Hell.

Not content with all this, however, the author now begins all over again, as though observing the same events from another viewpoint. Amid a positive nightmare of Great Beasts and seven-headed Dragons and Great Whores and demons and Antichrists and Armageddons—to say nothing of harvesting angels with sickles and the mysterious number '666'—doom is once again pronounced on the hated Roman Empire in terms so resounding as to reverberate right down to the present day with its terrifying images of the End Times, almost as though they threaten to engulf us as well.

As, who knows, if we convince ourselves enough, they well might.

None of this is dated, of course—indeed, had it been, we should by now be able to see perfectly clearly that it never in fact took place as predicted at all. Nevertheless, we should possibly beware—for history has an uncanny way of repeating itself (as **Nostradamus** himself clearly believed), while as-yet unfulfilled prophecies, similarly, display a worrying tendency to come true in the end in weird, perverted ways,[8] almost as though brought down on our heads, however unconsciously, by the very expectations of those who believe in them.

Whatever the truth of the matter, it seems clear that we should be well advised to treat the Bible's prophetic scenario, like the Hindu and Buddhist ones, as a kind of possible contextual backdrop, rather than relying on it too much for actual dates and details. That, after all, is what the *Little Apocalypse* was specifically designed for. As for the *Revelation of John*, this is a book of its time, designed for its time, and while we can apply it to our own times, too, if we wish, we have only ourselves to blame if we manage to frighten ourselves almost literally to death in the process.

St Malachy

Born in 1094 or 1095, the Irish monk and hermit Malachy O'Morgair rose to become Archbishop of Armagh before resigning in 1137 to return to his beloved contemplative life. Famed in his own lifetime for his healing powers and startling prophetic gifts, he died at Clairvaux in 1148 in the arms of his great friend St Bernard. Either on that occasion or during a previous visit in 1139 he is supposed to have composed a symbolic list identifying in advance all the one hundred and eleven Popes that he foresaw as reigning from the year 1143 until the eventual end of the papacy—symbolic in that each Pope is represented not by his name, but by a cryptic Latin tag or motto which could be interpreted in a number of different ways. True, the list was not finally published until 1595. This could conceivably explain why it successfully managed to identify the English Pope Hadrian IV (1154–9), who hailed from St Albans, as *De Rure Albo*, and Celestine III (1191–8), whose family name was Bonavensi, as *De Rure Bonavensi*. It could also explain why Alexander IV (1254–61), former Cardinal of Ostia, was listed as *Signum Ostiense*. Retrospective prophecy is, after all, not a new phenomenon, nor is it very clever.

Yet even allowing for the possibility of editing or forgery

in respect of Popes before 1595, the fact remains that the papal prophecies—whether truly by St Malachy or not—have indubitably been in existence ever since.

Not all of them, admittedly, have hit the mark—or at least, the link between prophecy and pontiff has sometimes been tenuous at best. Take the case of Pope Pius VII (1800–23), for example. This inoffensive cleric was, on the basis of Malachy's sequence, described as *Aquila Rapax* ('Rapacious Eagle')—which he was far from being. However, since he was dispossessed and imprisoned by Napoleon, the tag could well be seen as referring to the effective usurpation of papal authority by France's Emperor himself.

On other occasions, though, the prophetic bull's-eyes have been little short of amazing. Gregory XVI (1832–46) (*De Balneis Etruria*) was extraordinarily well described, being a monk at Balnea at the time he was elected, and an expert on Etruscan antiquities to boot. Leo XIII (1878–1903) was similarly well named *Lumen in Coelo* ('Light in the Sky'), both in terms of his incandescent spirituality and of his family coat of arms, which depicted a comet. The naming of Benedict XV (1914–22) as *Religio Depopulata* ('Religion Depopulated') seems appropriate in the light of the huge casualties of the First World War, while the saintly Pius XII (1939–58), formerly papal Nuncio to Germany, was not inappropriately called *Pastor Angelicus* (It. *nuncio* = Grk. *angelos* = 'messenger'). *Pastor et Nauta* ('Shepherd and Pilot') seems a perfectly apt description of his successor, the elderly but charismatic Pope John XXIII. He is best known, after all, for having steered and guided the Church into surprising new paths during the Second Vatican Council, whose chosen logo indeed included a ship. And if his successor, Paul VI (1963–78), was called *Flos Florum* ('Flower of Flowers'), at very least the prediction could be said to have been borne out by the floral design of his coat of arms.

The next Pope, the late John Paul I, was described as *De Medietate Lunae* ('Something to do with the middle of the moon'). In a book published in 1977,[11] I had already suggested that this might have something to do with the length of his pontificate. So, indeed, it did: he duly reigned for almost exactly a month. The present Pope, John Paul II, was described as *De Labore Solis* ('Something to do with the labour of the sun'), and turned out (less predictably, perhaps) to have worked in the open air in the stone quarries of Nazi-occupied Poland as a young man during the Second World War. In *Century* VIII.46 and elsewhere Nostradamus seems to refer to him by the same title (thus apparently suggesting that the Irish monk's predictions were, after all, already available for reference by the time of Nostradamus's death in 1566).

The predictions for the last two Popes of the series (yes, there are only two of them to go!) will be referred to in the course of the following pages, but it is clear even from those quoted that Malachy's papal sequence is well worth bearing in mind, even though it offers us no dates and may itself possibly have influenced the choices made by the various Vatican conclaves . . .

Nostradamus

Michel de Nostredame, the most celebrated French physician and occultist of his day, was born in 1503 in St-Rémy-de-Provence. A contemporary both of John Dee and of Paracelsus (to say nothing of the pioneering French writers Ronsard and Rabelais) he shared all his age's passionate enthusiasm for learning, philosophy, language, classical literature, alchemy and the other sciences both hermetic and overt. On the other hand, just as his unorthodox but remarkably successful methods of combating plague epidemics brought him into disrepute among the medical establishment, so his enthusiasm for the occult raised grave suspicions about him among the contemporary religious and legal authorities.

When, consequently, acknowledging his inherited gift of foresight and his expertise at 'scrying', he turned in his semi-retirement to producing annual almanacs and other books of prophecy, he chose deliberately to obscure the latter's language, lest he be persecuted by the Inquisition for practising black magic. Possibly, too, he preferred not to be accused of actually creating the dire events that he had foreseen by predicting them too clearly. Indeed, in the case of his most famous and explosive book, the *Centuries*, he even left its predictions in the self-same jumbled sequence in which he had possibly 'received' them in the first place.

The result is an infuriating hotch-potch of apparently unidentifiable verse-predictions (some 940 of them in all), full of obscure classical references and Latin and Greek borrowings, evidently written by a man who was thinking in Latin from the start, and juggling with his word-order with all the abandon of a Virgil or Ovid without even the benefit of the Latin endings which, in their case, were the only things that made their verses intelligible in the first place. The dedicatory letter to his patron, King Henri II, which accompanied later editions and purports to summarise their main predictions, is little better.

Most of the attempted word-for-word translations of Nostradamus, consequently—even those that have managed to achieve some semblance of linguistic reliability—have turned out (naturally enough) to be no more readable than were the originals.

What is worse, the resulting disassembled jigsaw puzzle (for that is more or less what it amounts to) has presented those who have preconceived ideas about the future (and which of us has not?) with a golden opportunity to indulge their passion for creating it anew in their own image. Picking verses here and there more or less at random, they have managed to read into Nostradamus's quatrains a whole range of past and future events to suit their particular fancies, from significant events in the seer's own lifetime on the one hand to the recent Cold War, the then supposedly imminent nuclear Armageddon between the countries of the Warsaw Pact and the West, the spread of AIDS, the deaths of the Kennedys and (so help us!) the lives of showbiz personalities such as Sean Connery and Michelle Pfeiffer on the other. Anything, in fact, which looms large enough in contemporary consciousness for somebody or other to ask the question: 'Surely he must have foreseen *this*?'

AVRIL.

De tous biens abondance terre nous produira:
Nul bruit de Guerre en France hormis seditions:
Homicides, voleurs, par voye on trouuera:
Peu de foy: fieure ardante: peuple en esmotions.

Augmentation de maladies	1	g ♍	14 Expeditiõ de classe barbari.
Mariage vidual arresté.	2	a ♍	27 Expediés pour apprehẽder.
Plusieurs bãdez contre trois.	3	b ♎	10 Vn entre autres captiué.
Retour de mauuais temps.	4	c ♎	22 ☉ à 2 h.40.m. aër turbidus
Hic ex pugna victor. magna	5	d ♏	5 Multorum grauis interitus.
Prelat & magist. desaccord.	6	e ♏	16 Mecaniq. & prelats brouillez
Deux fort grands d'accord.	7	f ♏	28 Australes procellæ vesperi.
Prelat discordãt à ij. grands.	8	g ♐	10 Frigidi venti cum plouia.
Trois grãds pmulg. de pred.	9	a ♐	22 Rois & Princes en bõ estat.
Presidẽs, Cõseillers par rois.	10	b ♑	4 Remis au magistrat.
Les grands Rois tous vns.	11	c ♑	16 Expedition barbarique.
Regi victori pax & securitas.	12	d ♑	29 ☽ à 5.h.13.m. Venti, imbres.
Pluie, changemẽt de temps.	13	e ♒	11 Amis entre ennemis liurés.
Aux occi. tout mauuais tẽps	14	f ♒	24 A custodia ad Gemonias.
Iuste vẽgeance de Dieu gai-	15	g ♓	7 Sterquilinium in aëre.
Profligez, bãnis, exilez. (deé.	16	a ♓	21 Ex amore furtiuo scandalũ.
Cerchant la vie, mis à vie.	17	b ♈	4 Le matin deliuré.
Venatio mota.	18	c ♈	18 Le grand peu fasché
Plages marines en frayeur.	19	d ♉	2 ☉ à 7.h.40.m. Vents.
Beaux & bons mariages.	20	e ♉	17 Beaucoup de biẽs aux fem.
Les anciens grands accord	21	f ♊	1 Auec tous infimes.
Trop bien aise tresmal.	22	g ♊	15 Freres vnis, sœurs non.
Tempeste, temps muable.	23	a ♋	1 Ruine redresse edifice.
Du pere au filz concordia.	24	b ♋	16 Thresor descouuert.
Temperature de temps.	25	c ♌	1 ☽ à 2 h 10.m. Pluie.
Dieu garde Liber.	26	d ♌	15 Tẽps louable nõ sans fraisch.
Affaire des fẽmes à rebours.	27	e ♌	8 Ambassadeurs ariuez
Despeche nouuelle, legatiõ	28	f ♍	11 Le tresdien venu & malade.
Infidelité d'esclaues.	29	g ♍	24 Fortercsses renforcees.
Conseil priué, remõstrance.	30	a ♎	7 Change les gardes.

Nostradamus's 1566 Almanac: predictions for April (by kind permission of Michel Chomarat, Association des Amis de Michel Nostradamus, Lyon)

Perhaps Nostradamus should have known better. Presenting the public with a jigsaw puzzle without the picture on the box was always asking for trouble—even though he did attempt to hint at such a picture in the two letters included in the editions that followed his death in 1566. The likelihood that anybody would ever sit down *without* such preconceptions and attempt patiently first of all to reassemble the jigsaw from first principles, and *only then* to hazard a guess at what it was all about, was, after all, a fairly remote one.

Yet it has been done. Two French commentators in particular—E. Ruir and Max de Fontbrune—seem to have had a fair stab at it during the late 1930s. Using a similar approach, and building on the extensive researches of more recent commentators such as James Laver and Erika Cheetham, I was able to publish in 1993 the first (and, to date, the only), English verse-translation of 430 or so of the prophecies arranged into a more or less continuous sequence of future events.[13] I did not, however, attempt at the time to date them.

I have since been able to supplement this with translations of over a hundred further predictions, *together with analyses of the relevant Nostradamian datings*. As luck would have it, these datings turned out to back my proposed sequence of future events almost to the hilt—though at the same time they demonstrated their supreme independence of my own views or wishes on the matter by mercilessly pinpointing half-a-dozen of the original predictions that I had inadvertently placed in the wrong order in the sequence, and two that didn't belong to this particular part of it at all.

Nostradamus, in fact, uses not one system of dating, *but three*. First, there is the approach based on the normal, familiar calendar. In the celebrated 72nd verse of his tenth *Century* (quoted on page 69), for example, he not only mentions the year '1999' in conventional figures, but specifies its seventh month.

For the most part, however, the seer seems to have felt that this system of year-numbering was inadvisable for his purposes. Possibly he suspected that it might eventually be replaced by some other—as indeed actually occurred at the French Revolution. An alternative, more arcane form of count tied to a known historical datum might allow him greater freedom to date his verses without revealing his hand too obviously. And so he devised his 'liturgical' count, which is mentioned specifically at verses VI.54 and (rather more obtusely) VIII.71.

While most commentators ignore this system, others have somewhat daringly attempted to decipher it. Some of them insist that it refers to the number of years since the influential Council of Nicaea held by the leaders of the early Church in AD 325. Others prefer to count (however ludicrous the idea may seem) *in months and days from the birth of Adolf Hitler in April 1889*. While both approaches produce (as almost any approach is likely to) some interesting 'hits', it has to be said that neither results in a very good over-all fit historically.

Which is not really so very surprising, given that neither event had anything to do with the establishment of the Church's liturgy, notwithstanding the Council of Nicaea's promulgation of the now-famous Nicene creed.

As was ever the case with Nostradamus, in fact, the answer comes only when one drops all preconceptions as to what it *might* be, and starts instead to look at the evidence strictly for what it is. It is simply a question, in other words, of investigating just when the Church's current liturgy was first laid down. There is absolutely no mystery about this.

Consequently I am able in this book to reveal for the first time the true basis of Nostradamus's 'liturgical' dating system.

It was in the year AD 392, in fact, that (on 8 November, to be precise) the Roman Church became truly Catholic (i.e. universal) for the first time, with the proclamation by the Emperor Theodosius I that Christianity was henceforth to be mandatory throughout the Roman Empire—and with it, inevitably, the so-called Canon of the Mass, newly drawn up by St Ambrose, which has remained at the heart of the Roman Church's liturgy ever since.

It is from the year 392, consequently, that Nostradamus's 'liturgical' dates have to be calculated—whether from January (as I have assumed throughout) or from November (which would effectively put back most of the resulting datings by one year).

This particular dating system is particularly prominent in his *Sixains*—a posthumous collection of 58 six-line verses that are so much more poetic in style than his earlier offerings (and so much easier to understand, too) that some commentators doubt whether he actually wrote them. Nevertheless, their themes do mesh in perfectly well with those of the *Centuries*, while their evidently 'liturgical' datings support the *Centuries*' chronology to the hilt. Both facts, then, argue for their authenticity. Possibly the *Sixains* are clearer simply because they were written in the seer's old age, and not intended for publication during his lifetime: he therefore felt free to use a more expansive verse-form that would allow him to say what he meant in normal French without fear of persecution, while actually dating much of it, too. Only the various players are somewhat coded.

Nostradamus's third dating system is purely astrological—or rather astronomical (for in his day the two sciences were indistinguishable). With its help, he claimed to be able to put a date on every one of his nine-hundred-odd quatrains. Nevertheless, he felt insecure about making his original predictions too easy to understand or verify. As a result, he was to date only a couple of dozen of his published verses in this way. (However, I have now succeeded in analysing these, too, this time with the help of the latest, computer-generated, planetary data from NASA's Jet Propulsion Laboratories.)

And indeed, had he used *only* this system for dating his predictions, the resulting information would not have been very useful to us, since the astrology of his day was based on the movements of only the sun, the moon and the five planets that were known at the time—namely Mercury, Venus, Mars, Jupiter and Saturn. Of these, the 'slowest' (because the farthest out) is of course Saturn, which is why it has immemorially been associated with Old Father Time. But since Saturn returns to roughly the same place in the sky every 29½ years or so, it follows that any datings based on the movements of the traditional planets alone will, in addition to being more or less cyclical, also be unlikely to be able to pinpoint anything much more precise than a selection of possible years within any given

29½-year cycle. Much, too, would depend on just how close any given generation of astrologers or astronomers expects phenomena such as planetary conjunctions to be.

This seems to be why Nostradamus goes out of his way (as we shall see) to use one particular year—namely 1999—to link all three systems together. The upshot is that it then becomes possible to fix his dates fairly positively for some centuries in either direction.

But this immediately poses an interesting question: *Why 1999, rather than some other year?* Evidently because the seer felt that events surrounding this particular year (which works out at '1607' by his liturgical count) would prove truly crucial—indeed, of such scope and magnitude as to dwarf anything that the world (or at least, *his own* world of southern France and Latin Europe generally) had ever known before.

I shall be investigating those events in the next chapter, which covers the years 1995–2000.

The total upshot for the current investigation, then, is an astonishingly detailed scenario for the next half-century and more consisting of over five hundred verses that not only refer, in many cases, to specific places and dates, but go on to describe the events involved repeatedly and in the most vivid detail.

This, of course, is ideal for our purposes, and I therefore make no apology for using Nostradamus's chronograph as a basic framework for the scenario outlined in Parts 2 and 3.

Quite how reliable we may assume Nostradamus's over-all picture to be naturally depends on just how accurate he has proved to be in the past. Unfortunately, thanks to the 'jigsaw-puzzle' phenomenon, estimates of this vary considerably. Sceptics, naturally, tend to dismiss him outright—not so much because of any perceived inaccuracy as because the very idea of prophecy conflicts with their rationalistic preconceptions. The typical, pick-'n'-mix approach of most would-be commentators, too, merely tends to discredit Nostradamus even further.

Perhaps, indeed, it is precisely because of this last phenomenon that, while most of the commentators themselves seem to assess his accuracy at between 80% and 90%, few of them agree with each other very often about just what it is that given verses are supposed to have been predicting. This, in effect, means that his reliability as perceived by the public at large is unlikely to be much greater than the commentators' own general measure of agreement—which probably works out as low as 10% or so.

While even this figure would, of course, be fairly remarkable, my own feeling is that it is vastly over-pessimistic. Like most individual commentators themselves, I suspect that Nostradamus's accuracy may well turn out to be in excess of 80%—though proving this will necessarily depend on how far one can successfully apply his prophecies to the future, rather than retrospectively fitting them to the past. I therefore propose to refer to my own version of his still-outstanding prophecies[13] in the pages that follow. This will provide an instructive test-case.

Edgar Cayce

Born in 1877, America's so-called 'sleeping prophet' received a very basic education in Hopkinsville, Kentucky, that set him on course to become a photographic darkroom assistant, and later a photographer and Sunday-school teacher. As a child, however, he discovered a remarkable gift for learning clairvoyantly in his sleep, as well as for diagnosing ailments and describing treatments—his own included—while in a kind of semiconscious trance. Later contact with a stage-hypnotist by the name of Al Layne helped to convince him that he could use this gift professionally for the benefit of others.

The outcome was the first of a long series of so-called 'health readings'. These he was able to give orally after putting himself into trance and being given no more information than an absent client's name and address. The results, taken down by a stenographer, were often so technically specialised as to prove totally unintelligible to Cayce himself when he regained normal consciousness, yet again and again the diagnoses were confirmed by doctors and the remedies proved effective. By the time of his death in 1945 some 14,000 stenographic readings had been amassed, and a research institute called the Association for Research and Enlightenment (A.R.E.) was duly set up at Virginia Beach, Virginia, to collate and publish them.

Long before this, however, the readings had taken an unexpected turn. From mere 'health readings' they had turned into 'life readings'. Not merely had Cayce started to speak of the past causes of illnesses in terms of his clients' former reincarnations (much to his own waking consternation as a Sunday-school teacher), but he had started to extend his revelations into the field of prognosis, too. And from there it was of course but a short step for him to foretell not merely the future prospects of individual clients, but to predict major future events in the history both of his nation and of the world as a whole.

Just like his health readings, then, these prophecies—famously convoluted and archaic though their style is—were duly collated and published by the A.R.E., and so we are able to make full use of them here. But it has to be said that many of those in respect of future events are rather unexpected, and often out of kilter with the revelations of other psychics. True, he successfully predicted the Wall Street crash of 1929, the USA's entry into the Second World War in 1941 and the defeat of the Axis powers in 1945. He similarly forecast the return of the Jews to Israel, the eventual collapse of Soviet Communism, an eventual renewal of freedom and spirituality in Russia that would become the 'hope of the world', and the beginnings of new links between East and West. Also anticipated were military conflicts in Libya, Egypt, the former East Indies, Syria and the Persian Gulf, as well as massive earthquakes on the west coast of America—these last having apparently been borne out in part by the huge Alaskan earthquake of 1964, as well as by more recent ones centred on Santa Cruz and Los Angeles.

In addition, Cayce forecast that at some date before 1998 the secret message of the Great Pyramid of Giza would be decoded—a prediction that was to lead directly to the writing of my own book *The Great Pyramid Decoded*[11] in 1977. By the same date, too, a secret 'Hall of Records' would be discovered near the Sphinx containing records and artefacts left there by the Atlanteans who, he claimed, had been the real designers and builders of the monument. And true it is that new, but so far unidentified, underground passageways and chambers have since been remotely sensed in the area by Japanese investigators from Waseda university using sophisticated sonic scanners.[12]

In all these respects, then, the Caycean omens are distinctly promising.

It was in the sphere of world-wide geological upheavals, however, that Cayce's predictions really started to run riot. Here, as we shall see, he went on to forecast huge earth-movements and subsequent widespread destruction not merely across North America, but in Japan and northern Europe too. Indeed, the earth's axis itself would eventually topple, with disastrous climatic consequences—and all this by around the end of the present century. That, at least, then, is a dating of sorts. And yet no other major prophet seems to forecast anything of the kind for the period in question.

What are we to make of this? There seems to be little sign of Cayce's Cataclysm *yet*—though, of course, it is not impossible. Yet it has to be said that it is in the sphere of datings that Cayce's revelations often seem to be least helpful—largely because he could rarely be persuaded to pin dates on specific events at all, and even then only in the vaguest terms. Sometimes, indeed, he took refuge in a version of the biblical quotation: '*But of that day and hour nobody knows, not even the angels in heaven, but only the Father*.' On other occasions he was merely woolly. Questioned about a world upheaval allegedly predicted by the Great Pyramid for 1936, for example, the sleeping Cayce offered, 'This is set for a correction which, as has been given, is between '32 and '38—the correction would be, for this—as seen— is '36,' while his dating for humanity's symbolic entry into the King's Chamber was given as ' '38 to '58' (compare diagram p. 10).

From the context, it is clear here that Cayce actually meant ***1938*** to ***1958***. This fits in fairly well with an important contemporary book on the subject by Davidson and Aldersmith entitled *The Great Pyramid: Its Divine Message*—which, in one edition at least, gives 1936 for the same event—but it is a good thousand years too early, if my own calculations are to be believed.[11]

A good many of Cayce's geological upheavals, similarly, were forecast to be already in evidence by the late 1960s. Yet they resolutely refused to occur. Some Cayce enthusiasts, consequently, felt driven to undertake a good deal of fairly energetic—not to say constructive—research in an effort to justify his claims. Following aerial surveys in the area of the Bahamas, for example, the Miami archaeologist Dr J. Manson Valentine actually dived on the Bimini reef in 1968 in an attempt to discover the remnants of the lost Atlantis that were supposed to be resurfacing in that year—and duly encountered, much to the sceptics' surprise, the whole complex of gigantic foundations that are by now a matter of public record.[1,11]

Clearly, then, Cayce had been justified. But then, from another point of view, he equally clearly had not. The ruins had been discovered, but they had not actually resurfaced as predicted. So should the idea of 'resurfacing' be understood here in some special sense? And if so, what of all his other as-yet unfulfilled predictions? Happen they undoubtedly may, even if in unexpected ways. But should not both Cayce's future predictions and the dates assigned to them really be understood in some special, symbolic sense—perhaps as *human* upheavals and topplings of *political* axes?

This raises the important question of just where Cayce got his information from. As he himself described it, it was as though he was being shown the information by some venerable sage on the 'other side' in the form of a kind of 'sacred book'. Enthusiasts for the esoteric will immediately recognise this as a picture of the activity that they refer to as 'reading the akashic record'. This latter is supposed to be a kind of indelible trace left on the fabric of space-time, or alternatively on the 'ether', by past events. Some of us, they claim, are sensitive enough to be able actually to 'tune in' to this record, whether in meditation or in dreams—and if so, then this is no doubt what Cayce, too, was up to.

This is theoretically fine as far as it goes, of course. But unfortunately it follows that if all past events are recorded in this way, then so, too, are all past ideas and theories—*including all the erroneous ones*. And if so, then this in turn might help to explain why so many of Cayce's ideas turned out in the event to be so strikingly reminiscent of the 'alternative' (and nowadays often somewhat discredited) theories of the 1920s and '30s—from the startling pronouncements of the contemporary pyramidologists on the one hand, via the favourite prescriptions of the dietary therapists and spinal manipulators, to the sweeping reincarnation-doctrines and prophetic cosmologies of the Theosophists and their ilk on the other.

In the light of this, then, we should probably be unwise to rely too much on Cayce's claims as a detailed guide to our immediate future, except in so far as they tie in with other sources of insight. He has, it is true, been remarkably accurate in the past, even in the matter of datings, but for the future he in any case offers us only a couple of true, dated 'appointments with destiny'—the one (as we shall see) for major spiritual developments in 1998 following his predicted period of huge geological disturbances, and the other for his anticipated planetary toppling, with all its further, massive geological and climatic consequences, which he dates to 2000 or 2001.

To which we could possibly add a vision of America shortly after the year 2100 (detailed in Part 3) that he had during a dream in 1936.

These are, of course, major prophecies, and well worth noting. But the rest of Cayce's revelations[2] are extraordinarily vague, especially where dates are concerned, and so are likely to be more useful to us as background information than as a primary source.

Possibly, though, we should always bear in mind his astonishing ability to surprise us.

Arthur C. Clarke

This eminent British science-fiction writer is an interesting and unusual case. Born in 1917, his first and possibly greatest claim to fame in the prophetic sphere was his publication in the issue of *Wireless World* dated *as early as October 1945* of a proposal for earth-orbiting communications-satellites to permit global TV-coverage. The idea has since borne fruit in a dazzling technological revolution that has totally transformed world-communications, possibly forever. Later, in 1947, he went on accurately to predict the first moon rocket for 1959 and—rather too conservatively, in the event—the first manned satellite for 1970 and the first moon-landing for 1978.

In his *Profiles of the Future*, published in 1973,[3] he went on to predict landings on other planets from 1980 onwards (the first Viking Lander actually touched down on Mars in 1976), personal radio for the mid 1980s and machine translation and fusion power for 1990 or shortly thereafter. All of these forecasts have duly borne fruit. On the other hand, forecasts (rather than prophecies) are in one sense precisely what they are. They are, in other words, more or less scientific and logical extrapolations—albeit aided by a prodigious imagination and freedom from prior conceptions—of what was already going on at the time of writing. Yet in another sense they have also taken on the quality of true prophecies, in that they themselves have tended to influence people's ideas, and thus arguably the events themselves.

Science-fiction writers such as Clarke, then, are not to be sneezed at (any more than H. G. Wells or Jules Verne) as possible sources of prophetic insight. Wells, after all, successfully predicted both the tank and aerial warfare, albeit rather close to the events themselves. As for Verne, he not only foresaw the long-range submarine: he also predicted, nearly a century in advance, a future moon-mission that would take off from the tip of Florida and eventually splash down in the sea . . .

Jeane Dixon

Undoubtedly America's most prominent seer and psychic of modern times, Jeane Dixon was born in 1918. Spotted as a child by a Gipsy fortune-teller, she was already advising people on coming events by the age of nine. Even while still at school she was consulted by numerous media personalities, and successfully predicted the election of Herbert Hoover as President. Subsequently she went on to combine work as a real-estate agent with frequent media appearances as a psychic, while at the same time displaying (like most major psychics) a profound spirituality—in her case rooted in her Roman Catholic upbringing.

So successful were many of Mrs Dixon's predictions that she was soon being consulted even by the great and famous. Before his death in 1945 she advised President F. D. Roosevelt (whose four electoral victories she had already forecast long before) that China would become Communist: it finally happened in 1949. She warned him, too, of a coming period of racial violence culminating in 1980. And when consulted in November 1944 by the dying President about his prospects, she told him that he had six months or less to live. He died some five months later.

Again, long before it happened she told Harry S. Truman, then wartime Vice-President, not only that he himself would become President but that—even more unlikely as it seemed at the time—he would be re-elected, too. By contrast, she advised Winston Churchill in 1945 that he would be defeated if he called an early general election in that year. He did, and was. But he subsequently returned to power, as Jeane Dixon had likewise foretold.

Elsewhere, she predicted to the year and month the dates of the assassination of Gandhi and the partition of India. For Russia she foresaw the replacement of Stalin's successor Malenkov within less than two years by a man with a goatee beard, who in turn would be overthrown by a short, bald man. Bulganin and Khrushchev duly fulfilled the prophecy to the letter. She also predicted the first Russian Sputnik and the subsequent unmanned moon-missions.

In 1961 she prophesied not only the death of United Nations Secretary General Dag Hammarskjöld in an air-crash, but also the suicide of Marilyn Monroe. She also prophesied, apparently like Cayce, the great Alaskan earthquake.

Most famously, however, she predicted in advance the assassinations of President John Kennedy, his brother Robert and the Reverend Martin Luther King, and did her utmost to warn all three in advance. She even managed a remarkably good stab at the name of the President's alleged murderer. Unfortunately, either the messages failed to get through, or the recipients determinedly took no notice of them.

But then possibly this was because she had by then started rather to discredit herself as a serious prophet, in some people's eyes at least, by unashamedly playing the 'media psychic'—successfully picking a winning raffle-ticket number when dared to do so, for example, or revealing on television, when challenged by Bob Hope, not only his golf-score that afternoon, but that of his unnamed opponent, whom she undiplomatically revealed to have been the then President Eisenhower.

Then again, she was occasionally all too fallible, and recognised herself to be so. Generally she put this down not to the quality of her often highly symbolic visions, but to her own faulty interpretation of them. Since the publication of most of her major prophecies in the 1970s that tendency has continued. A major failure, for example, was her prediction that a comet would collide with the earth in the mid 1980s—presumably the self-same major natural phenomenon that she elsewhere forecast as putting paid to a Soviet plan for world-conquest, while at the same time turning many people to Christ.

It is worth noting at this point, however, that Mrs Dixon distinguishes between two kinds of prophecy. There are, she suggests, Divine revelations on the one hand and mere personal visions on the other. The former are definite and irrevocable. The latter (the vast majority, it has to be said) are merely pictures of what is likely to happen unless people make the changes that are necessary to avoid it. To this extent, then, most of her prophecies should be regarded primarily as *warnings*—and highly useful ones, at that.

I shall be returning to this point in due course.

Jeane Dixon, in short, has to be regarded as a seer of the first magnitude, despite the distortions sometimes imposed upon her visions by her religious faith. Her over-all reliability may well be in the region of 80% or more. Consequently I shall be referring to her predictions[4] repeatedly.

Mario de Sabato

The illegitimate son of an Italian father and French mother, Mario de Sabato was born in Bordeaux in 1933, and discovered his clairvoyant gift at the tender age of seven. On his eleventh birthday he was 'recognised' as a future seer of world-eminence by a Gipsy fortune-teller, just as Jeane Dixon had been before him. It was 1962, admittedly, before he finally set up in business as a professional 'future-consultant', but thereafter his career went from strength to strength. By the 1970s (which is when most of his major prophecies were published) he was already being consulted by major political leaders. He was also lionised by the French press, who dubbed him 'the greatest prophet of the century' and 'the Nostradamus of modern times'. Estimates of his accuracy then ranged from 85% to 90%, and events since that time have not thrown those figures into too much doubt.

His claimed prophetic successes at the time included the Cuba affair of 1962, the Arab-Israeli war, the end of the Greek monarchy in 1967, the election of President Richard Nixon and the remarriage of Jackie Kennedy in 1968, the resignation of President de Gaulle in 1969, the election of Georges Pompidou to replace him, the deaths of de Gaulle and the Egyptian President Nasser in 1970, and the drama of the ill-fated—indeed, very nearly fatal—Apollo XIII.

Since that time his successful predictions (mostly written before 1971)[16] have included Britain's joining the EEC (which occurred in 1974)—albeit as a particularly 'difficult' partner—the Community's expansion to twelve or even fourteen members, the continuation of the Arab-Israeli conflict, the whole series of upheavals (both political and geophysical) that have dogged Italy ever since, the end of the Vietnam war (1973), the Ethiopian revolution of 1974, Turkey's involvement in a 'Cuba' affair with serious implications for international security (presumably its invasion of northern Cyprus in 1974), the withdrawal of President Gadaffi of Libya from direct administrative duties (1974), the restoration of the Spanish monarchy (1975), the subsequent reinvigoration of Spain's economy, the eventual Communisation of the whole of Vietnam (1976), the fall of the ailing Shah of Persia (1979), further troubles in Angola and the Congo, Russia's eventual reversion to capitalism (1991 onwards), enormous problems for a chaotic, post-Tito Yugoslavia leading to an influx of Russian troops and a European war, the eventual success of heart-transplant surgery, and even the advent of AIDS. True, he described the disease at the time as 'a kind of leukaemia'—but then it should be remembered that the HIV virus was indeed originally thought to be a leukaemia virus.

On the debit side, it has to be said that de Sabato announced that cancer would be defeated towards the end of 1975. He foresaw little success for King Juan Carlos of Spain in establishing a national government after the death of Franco. He predicted that Germany would never again be reunited—which has proved wrong in political terms, however right current political and economic difficulties are proving it to have been in spirit. And he seems at first sight to have misplaced the Gulf War by siting his predicted 'oil war' (during which oil-wells would be set alight, and in which Saudi Arabia would be involved) *in the Sahara*: on the other hand, there are signs that he may actually have been thinking in terms of a later war entirely . . .

No more than any other prophet, then, can Mario de Sabato be considered infallible. Like most seers, he seems to be at his most vulnerable when painting the larger picture. But then he himself is careful to point out that we are often faced with what he calls 'parallel destinies'. By no means all of the future is fixed and immutable. Much of it depends (as **Jeane Dixon** likewise points out) on the choices that we ourselves make. Manifestly, for example, King Juan Carlos made his own dramatic choice at the time of the abortive military coup of 1981 by courageously going on television and putting his own authority on the line, so saving his country for democracy. One of de Sabato's aims is thus to help us make those choices by warning us of the consequences should we fail to make the necessary changes: such was ever the function of the true prophet. And it follows that, if the prophet is successful in his task (as the biblical story of the morose Jonah illustrates to such hilarious effect), his direr warnings may in fact be proved not right, but wrong.

However, most people are not Juan Carlos. They can be relied upon not to face the challenge of destiny, even when warned. And so de Sabato's predictions to date have proved quite remarkable in their accuracy.

In the light of Mario de Sabato's obvious prophetic brilliance, English-speaking readers may be surprised at not having heard more about him—for the fact is that he has never (to my knowledge at least) been published in English. British publishers whom I long ago approached on his behalf (more or less as a *quid pro quo* for being permitted to report his predictions in my *The Great Pyramid Decoded* of 1977) seemed to feel that he would prove far too sentimentally autobiographical—far too *French*, in fact—for British readers. And true it is that the pious and frugal French seer has always worn his heart unashamedly on his sleeve, with human love and religious devotion very much his prime concerns.

However, such concerns are neither here nor there where prophetic accuracy is concerned. From this point of view the above list of accomplishments makes it abundantly clear that de Sabato is a prophet of the first order, and one whose predictions[16,17] we should do well to take very seriously indeed.

Other sources

By comparison with those just listed, it has to be said that most other prophetic sources pale into relative insignificance. This is not to say that they are necessarily invalid. But most of their predictions are either too few to evaluate, too vague to be of much use to us (even, alas, those of the Maya or the Hopi, to say nothing of the celebrated oracles of La Salette, Fatima, Garabandal, San Damiano and Medjugorje) or too wild and undisciplined to take seriously. In particular, dates are too often lacking.

Nor, in the past, have attempts to tie down the future by assembling whole panels of minor psychics or anthologies of their writings achieved much in the way of success. In the prophetic sphere, it seems, more does not necessarily mean better.

Not that there is any reason to pour cold water on alternative sources of prediction as such—except to the extent that prophecy is of course not a 'reasonable' activity in the first place. Indeed, the essentially intuitive and instinctive gift that is precognition is by no means confined to professional prophets. All over the world increasing numbers of minor psychics, whether published or not, are becoming sensitive to the drift of coming events as outlined in the following chapters. True, it is often difficult for less practised prophets to distinguish true, precognitive visions from mere everyday dreams, fantasies, paranoias and wishful thinkings. There is also a pronounced tendency for 'lay psychics' unconsciously to bring things forward in time, and so to spread unnecessary alarm and despondency abroad. Nevertheless, there can be no doubt about it—the dramatic events of the near future are already casting their dark shadow before them as they approach.

Formerly it was only the 'extreme sensitives' who were aware of that shadow—those 'long-range detectors' who are our major prophets. Now, however, perfectly ordinary people are starting to pick up on it, too. Some of them claim to be 'channels' for some kind of higher intelligence: others are prepared to accept full personal responsibility for what, in effect, is the activity of their own unconscious minds, possibly acting as a function of that greater Collective Unconscious whose existence was first posited by the great Carl Gustav Jung. Yet others merely admit to having unexplained hunches, and leave it at that.

And so it is that the celebrated words of the biblical prophet **Joel**, often applied to the coming Aquarian age, seem to be even now in the process of fulfilment: '*And it shall come to pass thereafter that I will pour out my spirit on all flesh; and your sons and your daughters shall prophesy, your old men shall dream dreams, and your young men shall see visions.*'

Even though I choose, then, to list in the ensuing Calendar for the most part only those predictions to which I can put a definite date, and to quote only those prophets who have a proven track-record, it is for you to ask yourself as you read them whether you, too, are not already subliminally aware of the general drift of coming events. Stay alive, too, to the premonitory feelings of others around you. And do not forget the messages that are constantly being beamed at you by the humble, everyday media. For, they, too, are sometimes more deeply aware than they realise.

In this way you will be able to validate for yourself—even if only fairly tentatively at this stage—the likelihood or otherwise of what I shall be proposing.

Until, that is, events themselves finally settle the question one way or the other.

Part Two

Calendar for a Generation

A WORD OF EXPLANATION

In Parts 2 and 3 you will find a comprehensive, dated calendar of events from 1995 until the year 4500. This is virtually unique within prophetic literature.

In Part 2 the calendar is divided into short periods of five years. In Part 3 much longer periods are addressed. For ease of reference, the period under discussion is also indicated at the top of each page. For each period a commentary is then supplied, designed to explain the background and point up the various themes and links involved. The commentary is further illustrated with maps and diagrams.

Basic to the calendar is the concept of the prophetic 'window'. This refers to the various dating-tolerances suggested by each prophetic source. Where, for example, a prophet predicts that a given event will occur 'in or after such-and-such a year', the sign ↓ is used: where he or she specifies 'by such-and-such a year', the sign is ↑. The sign ↕ indicates the mid-point between a starting-date and a finishing date. It is also used to indicate an approximate timing. Where a prophet indicates both the opening and the closing of a window, both are of course indicated at appropriate points in the calendar.

In a more general sense, too, ↓ also indicates a beginning, and ↑ an end.

Be warned, however. You may sometimes be faced with windows that, once opened, never seem to get closed, or with closed ones that you never realised were open in the first place. Some prophets, it seems, are much better at closing windows than at opening them. With others the reverse is the case.

Perhaps this is because the former are more concerned with simply revealing the state of affairs that is likely to have been achieved by any given date, while the latter are more concerned with dating the dawning of new human possibilities.

Perhaps, in other words, some prophets, having once established their viewpoint within the future, prefer to look back, while others prefer to look forwards.

It was ever so with human nature.

1995–2000

• DATE SUMMARY •

Arrows indicate the beginning ↓ and end ↑ of a prophetic window

1995	Oct (?)	Pope confirmed in office for five more years (*Nostradamus*)
1996	↑	End of especially dangerous period of international tension, with near-nuclear confrontation in Korea (*Mario de Sabato*)
1997	↓	Arab nationalists and/or North African Muslims commence violent anti-French activities (*Nostradamus*)
	Oct	New King accedes in Britain—or new President is installed in America (*Nostradamus*)
	↓	Greeks emerge from period of troubles, possibly at hands of Turks (*Nostradamus*)
	↕	Unidentified great siege: hostilities marked by war-crimes subside during winter, resume in spring (*Nostradamus*)

1998	↕	End of period of world-wide geological upheavals—American east and west coasts already flooded and Los Angeles and San Francisco destroyed by earthquakes; New York shortly to follow suit; Great Lakes draining southward into Gulf of Mexico; much of Japan submerged; much of northern European plain inundated (*Edgar Cayce*)
	↑	Reappearance of part of former Atlantis in area of Bimini, Bahamas (*Edgar Cayce*)
	↑	Rediscovery of Atlantean time-capsules in Egypt, Bimini and elsewhere (*Edgar Cayce*)
	↑	Return of 'Great Initiate', possibly as a spiritual influence rather than a physical person (*Edgar Cayce*)
	↓	Beginning of New Age of peace, scientific progress and developing human psychic gifts (*Edgar Cayce*)
	↑	End of five-year 'great crisis'; Chinese invasion of Europe (*Mario de Sabato*)
	June	Coronation of new British King(?) causes widespread rejoicing (*Nostradamus*)
	Aug	Central Asian Muslim powers start to invade Middle East (*Nostradamus*)
	↓	German Chancellor pays last visit to France (*Nostradamus*)
	Aug↓	Violent anti-French activities by Arab nationalists and/or North African Muslims increase (*Nostradamus*)

1998	Aug↓	Sudden destruction and war (*Jeane Dixon*)
1999	Feb	France and Italy start to be threatened (*Nostradamus*)
	Feb	Underground foundation of new 'kingdom of the spirit', or regime of psychic reintegration (*Great Pyramid*)
		Pan-Arab revolution overthrows Moroccan monarchy (*Nostradamus*)
	↓	African Muslim anti-French activities spread yet further (*Nostradamus*)
		Astrologers banned and persecuted (*Nostradamus*)
	July	Powerful new backer flies in to refinance temporarily defeated and stalled oriental advance; resumption of hostilities in Middle East (*Nostradamus*)
	↓	Start of Antichrist's reign (*Nostradamus*)
	↑	New form of electromagnetic energy harnessed (*Mario de Sabato*)
	↑	Major earthquakes damage nuclear power-stations (*Mario de Sabato*)
		European Union at height of powers, a year or so before final collapse (*Nostradamus*)
	↑	Revelation of already-present Messiah (*Mario de Sabato*)

2000	↓	Some kind of Divine intervention calls upon humanity to unite under a single God: cross appears in eastern sky (*Jeane Dixon*)
	↓	Chinese troops invade Middle East; huge battle east of Jordan; Israel temporarily spared (*Jeane Dixon*)
	↑	Unarmed Chinese invasion of Europe, while armed Chinese are attacking Russia (*Mario de Sabato*)
	↑	Artificial intelligence successfully developed (*Arthur C. Clarke*)
	↕	First space mission to colonise other planets (*Arthur C. Clarke*)
	↕	Development of remote energy-transmission (*Arthur C. Clarke*)
	↕	New understanding of atomic nucleus (*Arthur C. Clarke*)
	↕	New extensions of human perception (*Arthur C. Clarke*)
	↓	Earth's axis topples: severe geological disturbances; icecaps melt; sea-levels rise; possible alternative date for geological upheavals listed under 1998 above (*Edgar Cayce*)
	↓	Vatican becomes seat of new commission for peace and evangelisation: collegiate government replaces papal authority (*Mario de Sabato*)

2000		Pope delegates his powers to his cardinals—who use them to replace him with another (*Jeane Dixon*)
	Oct(?)	Pope forced to flee Italy by Asiatic invasion; comet appears (*Nostradamus*)
	Dec(?)	Pope dies near Lyon, France; comet disappears (*Nostradamus*)

•COMMENTARY•

SEERS AND PSYCHICS HAVE LONG BEEN VIRTUALLY UNANIMOUS IN seeing the end of the 1990s as an ever-darker period of confrontations, conflicts and potential international disasters. True, this is standard practice where ends of millennia are concerned. People expect the turn of a millennium to produce earth-shaking changes merely as a result of a new set of figures, rather as each New Year is heralded as portending the death of something old and the birth of something new, merely because the details on the calendar have changed.

Yet the prophets are remarkably specific in what they predict for the 1990s. They do not merely convey some vague feeling of impending doom. Some Roman Catholic seers, for example, go into considerable detail about what is to befall the papacy at this time, almost as though it were a kind of litmus paper for the wider changes in the world at large.

The future of the Popes

As noted in chapter 2, **St Malachy's** papal predictions offer a Latin description, or tag, for every Pope until the end of the papacy, and the various tags and Popes have long since been matched up with each other, often to quite stunning effect. On this basis the present Pope, John Paul II, was described as *De Labore Solis* ('Something to do with the labour of the sun')—a symbolic name which the later Nostradamus was likewise to take up in several of his predictions in the form 'Paul Mansol' (i.e. Paul *Manus Solis*, or 'Handiwork of the Sun'). It is to this Pope that *Century* V.92 then seems to apply, describing how 'after seventeen years' the papal term will be changed to five years instead of the present life-incumbency: at this point a new Pope will be elected who will in due course prove much less to the liking of the Roman Catholic Church:

Once he for seventeen years has held the see
They'll change the papal term to five years' time,
What time another shall elected be
Who with the Romans not so well shall chime.

Thus far, it has to be said, this particular prophecy has not been fulfilled. Since, however, John Paul II was elected as the 263rd Pope on 16 October 1978 (and enthroned on 22 October), he will complete the seventeenth year of his reign in October 1995—and (as we shall see) no subsequent Pope is likely to reign for anything like so long.

If **Nostradamus** is right, then, we are faced with the distinct possibility that on 16 October 1995 (or possibly 22 October) Pope John Paul II will be asked to stay on for a further five years. This does not necessarily mean that he will have offered to resign on the grounds of age or ill-health, still less that the regular papal term itself will at this particular juncture be changed from life to five years—possible though both outcomes are. Instead it may simply reflect official acceptance of the current Pope's already-expressed determination to lead the Church into the twenty-first century. However, the endorsement may or may not be made public.

On this basis, the Pope's reign would come to its natural close in the year 2000—were it not for other, truly dire events that (as we shall see) will prematurely bring about his death in that year. Verses such as *Century* VI.6 suggest that this latter will be marked by the appearance of a particularly bright comet:

Near Cancer's claws and the Septentrion
Of famed Great Bear, the bearded star appears
To Susa, Siena, Thebes, Eretrion.
Great Rome shall die the night it disappears.

Following this dramatic event, **Malachy** anticipates only two more Popes—*Gloria Olivae* ('The Glory of the Olive') and *Petrus II Romanus* ('Peter the Second of Rome'), who '*during the ultimate persecution of the Roman Catholic Church . . . shall feed his flock amidst many tribulations and, by the time these are over, the City of the Seven Hills shall be destroyed and the terrible Judge shall judge his people.*'

Nostradamus envisages much the same scenario in almost equally dramatic (and even more detailed) terms, while **Jeane Dixon**'s 1969 predictions[4] include the injury of one Pope in office (John Paul II was indeed severely injured by a Turkish would-be assassin's bullet on 13 May 1981), the enforced removal of another by the cardinals to whom he will have delegated increased powers, and his eventual return and assassination as the last Pope. **Nostradamus**, for his part, seems to identify the dispossessed and assassinated Pope as the present one rather than the last of the current series, but anticipates that the last two Popes, too, will be murdered in office, even if the Vatican is eventually to be restored after a gap of many years . . .

The end of the present papacy, then, is evidently for only two Popes' time, as is the destruction of Rome, and so it follows that the events precipitating both must already have had time to stir into action between now and then. It is these events that the prophets duly set out for the latter 1990s.

Premonitory rumblings

For **Edgar Cayce** this is primarily a period of major earth-movements, tectonic shifts, seismic catastrophes and floods. By the end of it, as our Calendar reveals, both the east and west coasts of the United States will (he says) be inundated, the cities of Los Angeles, San Francisco and New York will all have been destroyed by earthquakes and the Great Lakes will be draining southwards into the Gulf of Mexico instead of into the St Lawrence river—much as indeed seemed to be happening (seen from the air, at least) during the major Mississippi floods of 1993.

In particular, severe flooding connected with earthquake activity will have devastated the southern coast of California, southern Nevada and western Utah (especially, it seems, if Mount Vesuvius or Mount Pelée in Martinique have erupted in the meantime) while, in the east, South Carolina and southern Georgia will have disappeared beneath the sea, as will the coastal fringes of the states of New York and Connecticut.

Indeed, the only truly safe areas in the eastern part of the North American continent will be parts of coastal Virginia, Ohio, Indiana and Illinois, and southern and eastern Canada.

Elsewhere, South America will have been shaken from top to toe, while new land will have appeared off the south-eastern seaboard of the United States and off Tierra del Fuego, where there will be 'a strait with rushing waters'. Japan, long plagued by earthquakes, will have largely sunk beneath the waves. Much of the northern European plain, too, will be 'changed in the twinkling of an eye'—likewise overwhelmed by the sea—as will various of the battlefields of 1941 (which, for what it is worth, included Yugoslavia, Greece, Crete and the North African coast).

All this may seem distinctly improbable. Yet it has to be said that our ability to predict seismic events is still not well advanced. Nearly always they take us by surprise—so that (paradoxically enough) it would be no surprise at all if 'Cayce's Cataclysm' did, too. His view of our future world as one devastated by rising sea-levels and major inundations is, after all, no more than experts on global warming have long been warning us about.

On the other hand, the so-called 'Greenhouse Effect' is usually supposed to be a fairly gradual affair. Cayce's sea-level rises, by contrast, seem to be extraordinarily rapid. They are further exacerbated by a catastrophic toppling of the earth's axis in or shortly after the year 2000—the result of crustal disturbances at the poles which may be connected with polar melting and consequent weight-shifts. So vast and violent are the resulting upheavals as to beg identification with those predicted by the **Bible** for the dreaded 'Last Times'—the run-up to the end of the age and the long-awaited reappearance of the Messiah. '*Behold, Yahweh will empty the earth, split it apart, turn it upside down and scatter its inhabitants,*' warns **Isaiah** at 24:1. '*For the windows of heaven are opened and the foundations of the earth shake,*' he goes on at 24:18. '*The earth is shattered and broken apart. It is racked with convulsions and reels wildly. The earth will reel to and fro like a drunken man . . .*'

It all seems very scary if true, especially as the same chapter (24:4–6) also appears to predict other characteristics of our time, namely global pollution and possibly even such scourges as AIDS: '*The earth dries up and perishes, the whole world withers and sickens, the earth's uplands languish, and the earth is desolated by the feet of its inhabitants . . . For this reason a curse has devoured the earth and its inhabitants are aghast. Therefore the earth's populations dwindle, and few are left.*'

The resultant problem, it is worth noting, seems likely to be not so much *over*-population as *under*-population. Indeed, the admittedly Roman Catholic **Jeane Dixon** confirms specifically that the much vaunted population-explosion will simply not be an issue.

But then perhaps we should remember that major blights and pestilences are nothing new, and that although humanity's numbers may dwindle alarmingly as a result, it somehow always manages to survive them. Medieval Europe even managed to survive the dreaded Plague, after all, albeit at a cost of up to a third of its population. Moreover, one of those who did most to save his contemporaries from it was one of our own prime prophetic sources—the celebrated French seer and physician Michel **Nostradamus!**

Wars and coronations

Nostradamus's role at this particular point, however, seems to be to provide a rather less dramatic counterpoint to the major developments just described. Moreover, whereas **Edgar Cayce** is concerned primarily with events in America—in his case possibly pre-dated by a good many years—the more patient and precise French seer is concerned mainly with the future of France and Europe generally. And here he predicts a variety of apparently disparate events for the period.

At *Sixain* 14, for example, he describes a long-running war-cum-siege whose site he does not name, but which could apply as well to present-day Bosnia as to anywhere else:

More crimes the mighty siege shall bring,
Worse than before redoubling,
In '605 'midst verdant land.
Recaptured shall be what was ta'en,
Soldiers afield till frost's at hand,
Then, afterwards, afield again.

The circumstances are perfectly clear: brutal war will rage and territory continually change hands until winter puts a stop to hostilities, to be resumed again in the spring. If the verse does indeed refer to the former Yugoslavia—even, perhaps, specifically to Sarajevo—the pattern is a familiar one. The date, admittedly, lacks its initial digit—or rather the word 'mil'—but then this omission seems to have been almost as customary in French at the time as it is for us today to omit the first two. Moreover, in the *Sixains* particularly, it seems to act as a specific marker for **Nostradamus**'s 'liturgical count'. And in the present case this means adding 392 to 1605—*which works out at 1997*. At which point a further *Sixain* (No. 3) could well apply, too:

A thousand cannon-shots the town
Shall turn, remorseless, upside down,

With strong emplacements underground.
Five years she'll hold against such blows,
And then be handed to her foes;
Then, after war, with water drowned.

At *Sixain* 16 the 'liturgical' dates again refer to 1997 and 1998:

October '605 appoint
With royal chrism to anoint
Sea Monster's Steward, or exult
Should '606 in June befall
Great joys for lords and commons all:
Great deeds shall from that rite result.

However, this time the identities are even more veiled. 'Steward' (*pourvoyeur*) is a term that later predictions appear to apply to the USA in its role as provider of arms and supplies to a beleaguered Britain—itself, on the basis of other verses, almost certainly the 'great Sea Monster'—at a future time of dire conflict. Which suggests that the events in question could concern the unexpected inauguration of a new American President to replace a predecessor forced out of office in mid-term. On the other hand, the other details offered are distinctly regal—which makes it seem far more likely that the verse really refers to the accession in October 1997, and the subsequent coronation in June 1998, of a new *British royal* steward (i.e. a new King) who will go on to distinguish himself in a variety of ways. Possibly, then, it is significant that 1998 is the year in which the present Prince Charles will reach the age of 50.

In the hauntingly allegorical *Sixain* 18, which runs:

Considering the sad, Greek Nightingale
Who shall her woes with cries and tears bewail
And in such wise consume her earthly days,

Six hundred five she shall deliverance see
From all her pains: so does fate's web decree.
By means sinister she shall succour raise.

the reference is once again to 1997, and apparently to a new and better regime in Greece ('Philomelle' in the original). Threatened on her Thracian eastern frontier by the Turks (for the mythical Philomel was an Athenian princess who, violated by a Thracian prince, caused her own nephew's death and, as the nightingale, has mourned him ever since), Greece may find relief in that year when Turkey's attention is diverted to the increasingly critical situation now developing (as we shall shortly see) on her own southern and eastern borders.

And finally, at *Sixain* 19, we read:

In '605 and six and seven we
Until six hundred seventeen shall see
The ire, hate, loathing of the Firebrand spread.
So long beneath the olive tree concealed,
The Crocodile that lurks in fen and field
Shall rise to life, though he before were dead.

Here—there can be absolutely no doubt about it in the light of other references—**Nostradamus** is describing the irresistible, violent rise of Arab Muslim militancy and anti-European agitation after long centuries of torpor and relative subservience. This is destined to start in 1997, to spread rapidly during the next two years and to reach its peak in 2009.

Which brings us, inevitably, to the larger, long-term future of Europe and the Middle East as a whole.

The great invasion

Not all of it makes encouraging reading. Following the formation of a twelve- or fourteen-nation European Common Market, **Mario de Sabato** (writing in the 1970s) predicts left-wing take-overs in Italy, Portugal and eventually the United Kingdom, whose last King will be the present Prince Charles. Ulster—and eventually Scotland, too—will leave the United Kingdom. Following a hair-raising near-nuclear confrontation in Korea, the United States, stricken by severe financial problems, will decline in world-influence, though remaining friendly with Russia. Israel will constantly have to fight for its survival, with peace coming only when the Palestinians are finally granted their homeland.

But Mario de Sabato's most worrying predictions concern the rise of a great Arab prophet and conqueror, coupled with a vast Chinese invasion of Europe. The Chinese, he says, will start by attacking India. Later, the assault will resume much more seriously. After an initial move towards Japan, they will flood westwards through Indochina, India, Pakistan, Afghanistan and Russia, eventually overrunning Iran, Iraq, Syria, Turkey, Greece, eastern Europe generally, northern Italy, Austria, Germany, Switzerland, south-eastern France and parts of Belgium and Holland.

Yet it will be a largely benevolent invasion—or rather a migration. For the incoming hordes will for the most part be unarmed and unequipped, seeking merely to share in the riches of the West. Mario de Sabato refers, too, to their 'unshakable faith'—an expression which, it has to be said, seems to smack more of Islam than it does of Chinese Communism. It is in this and in their overwhelming numbers (half the home population) that their real power will lie. And the eventual upshot will be a mixing of the races and an entirely beneficial sharing of cultures. Indeed, the prophetic wisdom that the invaders are due to bring with them will to some extent succeed in saving Europe from itself.

But not before Europe has been economically ruined. True, the countries of far northern and western Europe will manage to stay more or less neutral, and so may avoid too much damage and suffering. Russia, on the other hand, will get itself involved in direct, armed conflict with Beijing, which (with American help) will subsequently be destroyed.

At the same time, however, Mario de Sabato expects the

whole of the Mediterranean basin and the countries bordering on it to be overrun by a kind of left-wing fascism which the by-then enlarged European Union will be hard put to it to repel—and then only with outside help either from America or from the Chinese themselves. France alone, he suggests, will be largely spared, because it will be the last to be affected and the least sympathetic to the ideas involved.

Jeane Dixon, too, expects a Chinese invasion, which (like **de Sabato**), she expects to start well before the year 2000, since she sees it being halted in the Middle East in that year—though she also foresees a new and more successful Chinese assault starting in the year 2025. **Nostradamus**, as we shall see, is more cautious: to him the 'Yellow Peril' is not necessarily Chinese at all (this suggests, by the way, that neither **Jeane Dixon** nor **Mario de Sabato** were much influenced by his predictions—which indicates an encouraging degree of prophetic independence on their part). True, he sees the invasion as emanating from the region of the former Mongol Empire (**Jeane Dixon,** too, sometimes uses the term 'Mongol'), and thus probably from somewhere in Central Asia—indeed, he also constantly uses the word 'red' of it—but at the same time he repeatedly describes it as *Muslim*, which would exclude most of China apart from the far north and west.

This point is a revealing one. What it suggests, after all, is that the real source of the mighty influx will lie somewhere within the newly independent Muslim Central Asian republics of the former Soviet empire, most of them still governed by former Communists. These include Kazakhstan, Uzbekistan, Kirgizstan, Tajikistan, Turkmenistan and Azerbaijan, with which we may also couple Afghanistan and Muslim north-west China—to say nothing of the other Muslim nations of the Caucasus and elsewhere within the Russian Federation. This is of course a vast area, inhabited—albeit relatively sparsely—by millions of devout and ever more nationalistic Muslims (at least 120 million of them speakers of interrelated Turkic languages) most of whom are tending to feel ever more resentful about their treatment at the hands of the former Soviet Union and suspicious of the intentions of its ever-more-powerful right-wing nationalists—and indeed of what they see as 'the West' generally.

Any further cultural or military threat, therefore—to say nothing of mass persecutions and betrayals such as that of the Muslims of Bosnia or Chechenya—may well result in a further increase in militant Islamic nationalism and regionalism throughout the area. In the power-vacuum left by the former Soviet Union, the field will then be clear for almost any local demagogue to offer himself as regional saviour, armed with simplistic, militaristic answers reminiscent of the former Genghis Khan—whose popularity, like that of the mythical Kirgiz national hero Manas, is indeed currently undergoing a tremendous revival.

In short, once the region has learned to exploit its own natural resources once more (with the help mainly of an ever-eager Turkey) the stage will be set for a vast military build-up. Matters military, indeed, are likely to be given precedence even over social welfare, to the point where they start to acquire a momentum of their own that could well wrest them out of the control of their original begetters.

The result could be a veritable *jihad* or 'Holy War' against the West, fuelled by a decidedly *un*holy mixture of cultural affront, vengefulness, fanatical—even suicidal—religious zeal and simple, traditional war-fever. As **Mario de Sabato** hints, sheer materialistic greed may well lure the Asiatic hordes westwards, too—for, to any oppressed and impoverished people, the now-widespread flaunting of Western riches and technology via Turkish satellite television must inevitably produce its effects in the end. And in all this the Central Asians are quite liable to be joined—given half a chance—by other militant Muslim states with cultural and religious axes to grind, notably Iran on the one hand and (especially) a still uncowed and defiant Iraq on the other. Indeed, new logistical links between central Asia and Iran (road and rail particularly) are already being forged, and both are forecast to be well advanced by 1996.

Perhaps it is not so very surprising, then, that at *Century*

V.25 **Nostradamus** forecasts the eventual defeat of Christendom by an 'Arab Prince' whom he refers to as the 'Coiled Snake'—a description which, curiously enough, has already been applied by the media to no less a person than Saddam Hussein. Forces nearly a million strong, he reveals, will invade Iran, before pressing on into Turkey and Egypt. And the astrology of the verse dates this initial development specifically to *21–22 August 1998*.

All of which naturally raises the question: 'But what are the Great Powers—and the West in particular—doing to allow all this?' The answer seems to be 'Minding their own business', for there are distinct indications in the various prophecies, and notably those of **Nostradamus**, that the present trend towards regional isolationism is likely to increase as the decade wears on. Especially does this seem to be the case in the USA. Nations and power-blocks will become ever more inward-looking, ever more reluctant to get mixed up in other people's quarrels or to commit their young people to wars that do not seem directly to concern them. Concerted action, consequently, will become ever more difficult to organise.

True, there will be talks and conferences. **Nostradamus** foresees a visit to Paris by somebody who looks remarkably like Germany's Chancellor Kohl, using an abbreviated form of his already explained 'liturgical count' to date it to some point between 1998 and 2001. It seems, however, to be the Chancellor's last political act (*Sixain* 25):

Six hundred six or nine are for
A great ox of a Chancellor,
A Phoenix old and full of years.
His face no longer here shall shine:
From state his mem'ry shall decline.
On Champs-Elysées he appears.

For all the talk, however, little will be done. As in present-day Bosnia and pre-Second-World-War Czechoslovakia, events in the Far and Middle East will be seen as pertaining to far-away

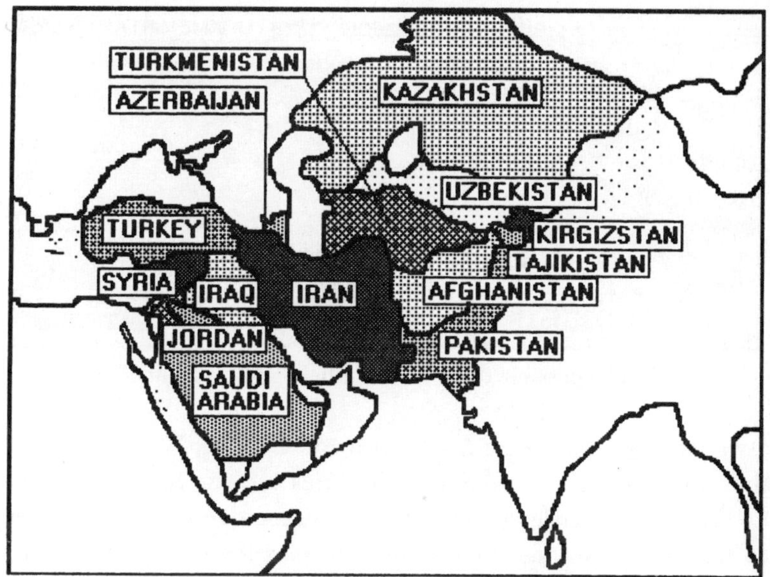

The main Muslim states of western and central Asia

countries of which we know little. Diplomatic myopia—shutting one's eyes to foreign realities, at least outside one's home area—is likely to become a required skill among politicians of all persuasions. As **Nostradamus** suggests at *Century* II.39, the politicians of the European Union especially are much more likely to be focusing at the time on further steps towards integrated internal power-structures than on ever more threatening events wider afield:

A year before war comes to Italy,
French, Germans, Spaniards shall think might is right.
When falls their infantile republic, see
How most of them are choked to death by might.

And so it is that, by mid-February of 1999, with militant Islam now rampant throughout the Middle East and North Africa, **Nostradamus** sees the storms of war set to sweep into the Levant, their ripples already washing on to the unsuspecting, far-

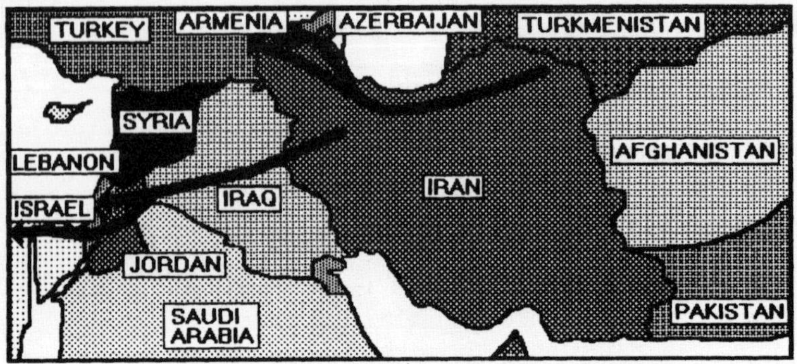

The possible route of the initial Asiatic advance

away shores of a sleepy Mediterranean Europe. With Jupiter at the 'point of Aries' and Saturn in Aries too (he reveals at *Century* I.51), immense changes both in France and in Italy are set to mark a new stage in the ancient astrological cycle, as bad times return to the Mediterranean countries generally:

Saturn and Jupiter in Aries met:
Eternal God, what changes are in train!
In France and Italy what stirrings yet
As the slow round brings evil times again!

And it is worth pointing out that, when **Nostradamus** says 'changes', he normally means disasters (a term which, after all, originally meant 'derangements of the stars').

The Nostradamus scenario

Of all the prophets, it is **Nostradamus** who describes the coming invasion in by far the greatest detail. His portrayal is dramatic, vivid, even terrifying—so much so as to bear comparison with the most extravagant pictures painted by the religious doom-mongers or even the science-fictionists. Yet at the same time it is astonishingly specific, too. Unlike most other seers he names names, pinpoints exact places. Sometimes he fixes precise years, even in some cases actual months and days.

Of all those dates, however, Nostradamus seems, as we saw in Part 1, to have felt that the year 1999 was the most crucial. The predictions outlined on the following pages will begin to suggest why this should be. Some of them (especially those that are rarely published at all) are quoted here in full, while the rest are merely listed: most of these are to be found in my earlier book *Nostradamus—The Next 50 Years.*[13] The few that are not may be found in a variety of popular editions, notably Erika Cheetham's *The Prophecies of Nostradamus* (Corgi, 1975), the same author's *The Final Prophecies of Nostradamus* (Futura, 1990) or Henry C. Roberts's *The Complete Prophecies of Nostradamus* (Grafton, 1985).

The Asiatic hordes have by now ensconced themselves firmly in the Middle East (*Century* V.25). There are signs elsewhere in Nostradamus that a kind of triple confederacy has been cobbled together between the Central Asian republics, Iran and Iraq. Most of Turkey is already firmly under the heel of the invader (VI.55, V.86, I.40, V.27, III.60). Now the attack is about to turn on Israel (VIII.96, V.96), while ahead of it the tentacles of fundamentalist Islam are starting to strangle more moderate Arab regimes all along the North African coast from Egypt to Morocco. As a result (as VI.54 reveals), in 'the year 1607 of the Liturgy' (i.e. 1999) simultaneous risings are set to occur in Tunis, Fez and Bougie or Bejaia (Algeria), with the King of Morocco deposed and imprisoned by Arab militants. Indeed, the French seer is even more specific: clearly the event is one that he has not only 'seen', but 'heard'. The rising, he says, will start at break of day, just as the cock is crowing for the second time.

Possibly it is at this point that more civilised voices in the Middle East seek to warn the West of what their more hot-headed countrymen are about to undertake. As Nostradamus puts it at *Sixain* 8:

The coming business just before
From Persia an ambassador

Shall come to France with word of it.
In vain his hopes; rejected he:
Of Allah downright blasphemy
When he shall feign his God to quit.

An Islamic envoy who is prepared to abjure his faith is evidently not regarded as having very much credibility, even in the West.

Soon, however, the truth of the unwelcome message starts to dawn, and alarm and despondency now spread throughout Western Europe. Popular soothsayers and doom-mongers, consequently, are soon having a field-day, while traditional religion is falling by the wayside. No wonder that at least one government tries to stem the flood of alarming literature by persecuting and outlawing astrologers and subjecting their writings to ridicule (*Century* VIII.71). (It may not be possible to magic the facts away, in other words, but at least it is possible to gag the messengers.) Nostradamus does not name the country concerned, but he does give a date. This development, too, it seems, is due to take place in the 'year 1607 by Church's count'—i.e. the fateful 1999.

A light in the darkness

At the same time, though, there are much more hopeful signs, curious though they may seem at this juncture. Some of them are scientific, some spiritual, others purely military. For a start, the invaders suddenly suffer a major check somewhere in the Middle East. **Jeane Dixon** suggests that they will actually be defeated in Palestine, somewhere east of the river Jordan. **Nostradamus**, for his part, suggests that they will have run out of money and supplies. He also hints that their leader will suddenly have died. Whatever the truth of it, there is an unexpected pause in hostilities, and out of the darkness shines a temporary gleam of light.

For **Arthur C. Clarke**, it seems, that gleam involves likely advances in the fields of artificial intelligence, space technology, world-communications, energy distribution and subnuclear physics. New developments in electronics, in particular, promise nothing short of a new Golden Age, with almost unlimited possibilities for humanity. **Mario de Sabato** even predicts the harnessing of some new kind of electromagnetic energy with important implications for space-travel—though the other prophets place this development a good deal later.

'Barring war,' writes **Clarke,**[3] 'this Age lies directly ahead of us.' As we have seen, however, war seems likely to be far from barred, and so heaven may well have to wait a while.

But Clarke also envisages new advances in human perception, and here his insights start to mesh in with those of other seers of a more spiritual and less overtly scientific cast of thought. For several of our prophets, after all, the gleam of light that starts to shine forth in around 1998 or 1999 is essentially spiritual in nature. Whether, with the **Great Pyramid**, we see it merely as the initial spark of better and more enlightened times or, with **Edgar Cayce** and **Mario de Sabato**, as the biblically predicted lightning-flash actually accompanying the advent (whether in the flesh or merely in the spirit) of the long-awaited Messiah and the Kingdom of Heaven on earth, is a question to which we shall be returning later.

Nevertheless, things do seem to be moving in this area. **Edgar Cayce**, like **Jeane Dixon**, foresees a new growth in human psychic powers, very much along the lines of the prophet **Joel**'s prediction in the **Bible** (quoted at the end of Chapter 2 above) of an outflowing of the Holy Spirit, of a dreaming of dreams and a seeing of visions. But at the same time **Cayce** is careful to couple this with new advances in the scientific sphere, aided by new discoveries of ancient Atlantean artefacts and records concealed in the various time-capsules that he expects to resurface at this time. In particular, he seems to suggest, we shall rediscover the secret of the Atlanteans' 'Great Crystal', which was allegedly able to capture, convert and beam solar energy directly to users all over the earth.

This idea may seem fanciful in the extreme. Curiously enough, though, it is very much in line with at least one development that **Arthur C. Clarke** expects to see during the very period under discussion—namely the direct beaming of energy to remote users.

Cayce's proposed alliance between spirit and matter is a truly vital one, and one that the Atlanteans (he suggests) had long mastered. It was only when the link broke down that they brought about their own final self-destruction in around 10,000 BC. No doubt that is a lesson from which we might all profit. For destruction seems to stare us in the face, too, and for very similar reasons.

Yet somehow, as **Jeane Dixon** seems to hint (even if not consciously to realise), there will actually be hope in that very destruction. For her oriental invasion is dated to the very same year as her great cross in the eastern sky and her 'Divine intervention' that calls upon all humanity to unite. In destroying the Old Order, in other words, the invaders will be clearing the ground for the eventual foundation of an entirely new one, much as **Mario de Sabato** specifically suggests—or, as the ancient Hebrew prophets would have put it in their characteristically topsy-turvy way, in 'punishing the wicked' the enemy will be acting as the very instrument of God.

Exactly—curiously enough—as the Islamic invaders will themselves be claiming.

It has been the Old Order's very determination to cling on to all its old habits and iniquities, its assumptions and delusions, in fact, that has prevented the very improvement to which it has claimed to be committed. As folk wisdom prefers to put it, you can't have your cake and eat it too.

The assault resumes

But then impending events, it seems, are about to scotch both proverbial possibilities anyway. Suddenly some unidentified national leader with an ideological axe to grind flies in to refinance and resupply the stalled oriental campaign. Newly supplied with arms—and particularly with the ships (possibly mothballed vessels purchased from Russia and/or the Ukraine) without which it cannot easily advance into Europe—the great westward march can continue. And immediately the fat is once again in the fire.

It is to this situation that the celebrated 72nd verse of **Nostradamus**'s tenth *Century* now refers:

Let 1999's seventh month arrive,
Then comes from heaven a great financing lord
The Mongols' mighty leader to revive.
War reigns before, then haply is restored.

Note that the 'financing lord' (or 'King-Paymaster') concerned is popularly misinterpreted as a 'King of Terror' (the term *Roy d'effraieur* seems to be merely a typical Nostradamian 'blind' for *Roi deſfrayeur*). But then who is to say whether he might not be that as well?

At once a new oriental leader emerges whom Nostradamus seems to identify as the biblical Antichrist in person (V.55, V.84, X.75, X.10). Once again using an abbreviated version of his 'liturgical count' (one which, as we have seen, takes the initial thousand as already read), he describes how in 1999 the great oriental tyrant is about to advance into Europe, driving before him one particular Western leader (possibly British) whom he characterises as the 'Leech'—i.e. either a bloodsucker feeding on the less fortunate, or (at best) a somewhat inferior healer of the world's ills (*Sixain* 21):

The Author of all ills shall rule
From '607, a monster cruel
To those o'er whom the Leech shall reign.
Then step by step he shall advance
To light his fire right here in France,
While Leech returns back home again.

And so it is that Nostradamus warns the 'Griffon'—the composite creature with which he symbolises the disparate nations of the Western European alliance—to rearm in the face of the advancing 'Elephant' of vast (and growing) Middle Eastern and Arab aggression (*Sixain* 29). Once again he uses his 'liturgical' count to date the relevant verse to the year 1999, at the same time warning of some horrific new maritime weapon that will set the very sea alight—unless, of course, the reference is merely to some kind of disastrous spillage of oil:

Let Griffon now himself prepare
To fight the foemen everywhere,
And let his army strengthened be;
Or else the Elephant shall him
Surprise with sudden force and grim.
Six hundred seven burns the sea.

Evidently the warning goes largely unheeded, though. By the latter end of the year 2000 the swarms of invaders—relatively disorganised though they are at first—have already succeeded in entering the Balkans (*Century* X.58), have laid waste much of Greece (V.90, V.91, IX.91) and Yugoslavia (II.84, IX.60, II.32, IX.30) and have even started to attack Italy's north-eastern borders (II.33, I.9), as well as its southern and eastern coasts (I.9, VIII.84). Both Venice (III.11) and Vicenza (III.75, VIII.11) are soon at the invaders' mercy.

Huge battles follow in the north-east near the mouths of the rivers Adige and Po (II.43, II.33). The victorious invaders start to swarm westwards—like locusts, as both the **Bible**'s *Revelation of John* and **Nostradamus** put it—across the Plain of Lombardy (IV.48), as well as up the Danube into Hungary (*Présage* 31, *Centuries* V.48, X.62, II.24, X.61, II.90, VIII.9) and through the Alpine passes into Switzerland (II.96, IX.44). After daring sea-borne invasions of Sicily, Corsica and Sardinia (II.100, VII.6, VIII.84), and amphibious landings between Ancona and Rimini (III.21, II.5), the south of Italy, too, is soon overrun.

The 'locusts' reference is particularly interesting. The way in which **Nostradamus** uses the term (which he sometimes replaces by the word 'grasshoppers') suggests not merely 'marauding hordes', but actual winged cavalry, much like those described by the **Bible**'s *Revelation of John* (9:3, 7–10). In the light of this it is tempting to wonder whether the seer has actually 'seen' squadrons of modern helicopters descending from the sky. And if the French seer, then what of John himself? He, after all, describes specifically the noisy whirring of their wings (9:10).

Indeed, John's *Apocalypse* then goes on to relate something that seems disturbingly close to likely reality (9:14–19). '*Release the four angels that are penned in by the great river Euphrates*,' commands a heavenly voice at this point—though other contemporary apocalypses refer to 'four kings', thus begging identification with the present-day leaders of Iran and Iraq, plus two other Asian states. '*So the four angels that had been held ready for this very moment—even for this very year, month, day and hour—were released to kill a third of humanity. And I heard the number of the squadrons of their cavalry: it was two hundred million. And this was how I saw the horses in my vision . . . the horses had heads like those of lions, and out of their mouths poured fire and smoke and sulphur . . . their tails were like snakes whose heads were just as noxious*.'

If helicopters, then, what price tanks, flame throwers, even guided missiles?

Meanwhile, if such vast and powerful forces are indeed in play, perhaps it is no wonder that **Nostradamus** now describes by name the fall of town after town, city after city. Soon Rome itself is under attack (*Centuries* II.43, VI.20, VI.25, I.11, VIII.62), and it is at this point that he sees the Pope (apparently, as we have seen, the now eighty-year-old John Paul II) fleeing via one of the Alpine road-tunnels (V.57) to meet his death in France's Rhône valley (VII.22, VIII.46), somewhere near Lyon (II.97).

The Pope goes to meet his fate

As *Century* X.3 puts it, by the end of his renewed five-year lease the elderly pontiff will no longer be 'feeding his flock'—

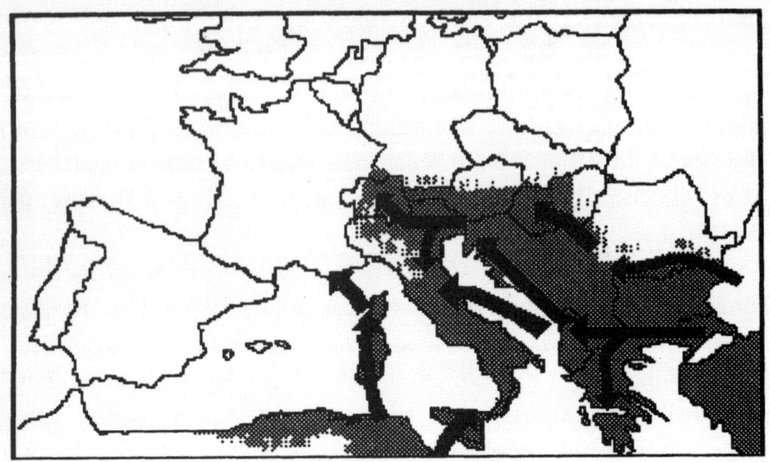

The Muslim advance into Europe

i.e. adequately discharging his responsibilities as leader of the Church. Amid rumours and counter-rumours of help from abroad, there are mysterious hints of an attempted undercover deal apparently involving the freeing of a fugitive with Polish connections. Then the Pope finally flees Rome (II.41), his flight marked by the baying of some unidentified mastiff (elsewhere **Nostradamus** seems to use the term to refer to the invaders' chief spokesman, or even to their supreme commander).

More strikingly, though, the papal flight will also be marked (as we have already seen) by the appearance of a brilliant comet in the night sky—so brilliant as to outshine the very sun itself (*Century* II.41 and C VI.6, quoted on page 53 above). The phenomenon, first appearing in the area of Cancer and the Great Bear, is destined to show particularly vividly over Italy and Greece, and will last for all of a week—but by the end of it the old man will be dead. He should be particularly wary, Nostradamus warns at II.97, of seeking refuge in the French city of Lyon, for the 'blooming of the rose' (a flower which the seer often associates with the 'red' invaders themselves) will see both him and his party coughing up their lifeblood in the vicinity.

For Nostradamus, evidently, this whole event is an important one, and vastly symbolic for the future of Catholic Europe. It presages the eventual, abject collapse of Christendom in the face of militant Islam, and with it not the gentle benevolence of **Mario de Sabato**'s migrating Chinese, but the destruction and desecration of Western Europe itself.

As a weak, vacillating and possibly collegiate regime takes over in the Vatican (VII.23)—a collective regime also presaged by **Jeane Dixon** and **Mario de Sabato**—desperately trying to stave off the worst by buying the enemy's goodwill with acts of covert co-operation, the invaders are pressing on remorselessly with their campaign of anti-European vengeance. As Pope succeeds Pope and canny ecclesiastical fraternisation turns to blatant corruption (VIII.20, V.49), there is little that the Italians can do, even with belated French help, beyond slowing the advance as best they can.

After the fall of both Naples and Rome, the defenders suffer a further huge defeat at Perugia (VIII.72). Florence and Lucca are not slow to follow (VII.8, VI.62, III.19). At the same time a mounting tide of sea-borne attacks starts to affect the Italian and French rivieras (X.60, IX.42, II.4, IX.61, III.10, III.82).

Pause for thought

For some years, then, the southern Europeans seem to be in for a thoroughly bad time of it, as **Nostradamus** has already foreshadowed in *Century* I.51 (see page 64 above). So bad, in fact, that it will all be well nigh incomprehensible to them. Ever since the Renaissance, after all, the established wisdom has been that humanity is basically perfectible, even if not yet actually perfect. Human beings, far from being the wretched, vice-ridden, all-but-irredeemable worms of medieval tradition, have it within themselves to be positive giants, or even gods. They can, if they choose, be masters of the universe, arbiters of their own destiny, creators of their own moral law.

Humanity, on this model, is basically good. And no wonder. All the darker aspects of human existence, after all, have been deliberately banished to the shadows. Poverty and unemployment have been largely exported to the Third World. Hunger and disease have been packed off to keep it company. Inborn racism has been exorcised simply by keeping the 'aliens' safely at home, while destroying their civilisations for them in the name of progress. War has increasingly been exported to foreign battlefields and countries far away.

Our world, in short, is nice. People are nice. The universe is nice. And by rights nothing nasty ought ever to happen to us.

And now, suddenly, all that seems set to change. Our whole civilisation seems set to be torn apart. The poor and hungry, the racists and plague-bearers, the bringers of death and destruction are set to descend on us from 'out there'—as indeed our problems always do when we deny their existence 'in here'.

And as a result we, too (even the most benign and pacifist of us), are likely to have to fight—not merely for our civilisation, but for our very lives and families. In the process we shall no doubt be shocked out of our minds by the sheer intensity of *our* hitherto-hidden feelings of aggression and hatred, *our* yen for tribalism and xenophobia, *our* capacity for cruelty and contempt. For if **Nostradamus** is to be believed, the conflict will make the last two World Wars look positively gentlemanly. Especially as it spreads into southern France and then further northwards, no quarter will (as we shall see) be asked or given. The invaders will prove unstoppable. Deterrence will be of no avail. From the Mediterranean in the south all the way to the Danube in the east and (it seems) eventually the Rhineland itself, huge numbers of fanatical, even suicidal Islamic shock-troops are set to destroy everything in their path. Rampaging their way throughout almost the whole of Latin Europe, they will torture, kill and rape with complete abandon (and with complete disregard for everything that Islam ever taught), while spreading the most horrific forms of disease both deliberately and by accident wherever they go.

And we 'cultured' Europeans, for our part, are likely (much to our surprise) to find ourselves retaliating in kind.

In short, brute, barbaric medievalism is set to rear its ugly head once more. And, worst of all, a truly dire lesson is about to force itself upon us—namely that people are not nice after all. Not 'them', not even 'us'. Instead, we are all at heart extraordinarily . . . well, *medieval.*

It cannot help but come as a terrible shock to us, and a devastating blow to our nice, comfortable illusions. Notwithstanding the clear evidence that has emerged quite recently from the troubles of Northern Ireland and Bosnia—to say nothing of the murky facts about the human psyche long ago dug out by psychologists such as Freud and Jung—we shall be faced with the hard reality that people (Muslim and Christian alike) are both cruel *and* kind, both virtuous *and* vicious, both moral *and* depraved, both generous *and* self-obsessed, both cosmopolitan *and* racist, both spiritual *and* materialist, both cultured *and* profane. In short, I am both mind *and* body, both spirit *and* animal, both 'I' *and* me.

It is not a question of either/or. It is not even a matter of 'the rotten apple in the barrel'. *All* apples have it within them to be rotten, just as all apples have it within them to be pristinely fresh. Neither is the 'true' state of the apple. It depends entirely on when you look at it.

And possibly it is in learning that lesson that we shall take the first step towards what the **Great Pyramid** sees as our eventual attainment of a more truly whole and integrated consciousness.

Our illusions, in other words, *have* to be shattered. And since we have spent the last few centuries in particular doing everything we possibly can to ensure that nothing of the kind ever happens, the pressure for that shattering to occur has built up to incredible levels. As a result, some kind of communal catastrophe is virtually inevitable—a catastrophe which, however painfully, will eventually lift the veils and reveal to us both ourselves as we truly are and our world as it truly is.

Not a world that is wholly good, nor a world that is wholly bad, but a world that is whole and perfect and exactly as it has to be. A world that, in reality, is as it always was and always will be. A world that, in consequence, will at long last cease to war and struggle and fight unceasingly over what it in theory *should* be.

Moreover, as ever, that catastrophe has to come from precisely where we banished our darker side to in the first place—namely from the long-suffering Third World. The result has to be a world crisis of the first order. And it is the Muslim invasion of Europe that is, it seems, destined to supply it.

2001–2005

• Date Summary •

Arrows indicate the beginning ↓ and end ↑ of a prophetic window

2001	↑	Last likely date for German Chancellor's final vist to France (*Nostradamus*)
	↑	Last likely date for toppling of earth's axis, melting of icecaps, rise in sea-levels and geological upheavals listed under 1998 and 2000 above (*Edgar Cayce*)
	Jan	New Pope elected, destined to betray the Church (*Nostradamus*)
	Mar↓	Possible start of era of destruction and/or total collapse of materialist societies (*Great Pyramid*)
	Mar	Possible alternative date for papal election above (*Nostradamus*)
2002	May	Islamic forces victorious in Italy and Greece (*Nostradamus*)
	June↓	War resumes in Italy (*Nostradamus*)

2002		Rome under renewed attack (*Nostradamus*)
		Invaders start to turn their eyes towards France (*Nostradamus*)
2003		War-conference of invading commanders near Venice (*Nostradamus*)
2004	↕	Mid-window for start of era of destruction and/or total collapse of materialist civilisation (*Great Pyramid*)
	Aug	Severe earthquakes and tidal waves in eastern Mediterranean, notably Greece and Turkey (*Nostradamus*)
	Dec	Economic collapse of northern Italy and most of Western Europe (*Nostradamus*)
2005	March	Invading forces withdraw to central Italy to recuperate (*Nostradamus*)

•COMMENTARY•

THE TWO MIGHTY PINCERS OF THE MUSLIM LAND-BORNE INVAsion have now finally closed on north-western Italy from Pisa in the south to Milan, Pavia and Turin in the north. Now the rest of **Nostradamus**'s prophecy will no doubt follow, too. The French, aware as never before of the looming threat to their own country, will hurriedly withdraw their expeditionary forces, no doubt foreseeing a more effective role for them in stopping the enemy in the narrow passes along the Mediterranean coast and through the Alps.

And so it is that the whole of Italy eventually falls, and a shocked Europe stands aghast as the call of the Muezzin echoes eerily over formerly Catholic rooftops all the way from Palermo

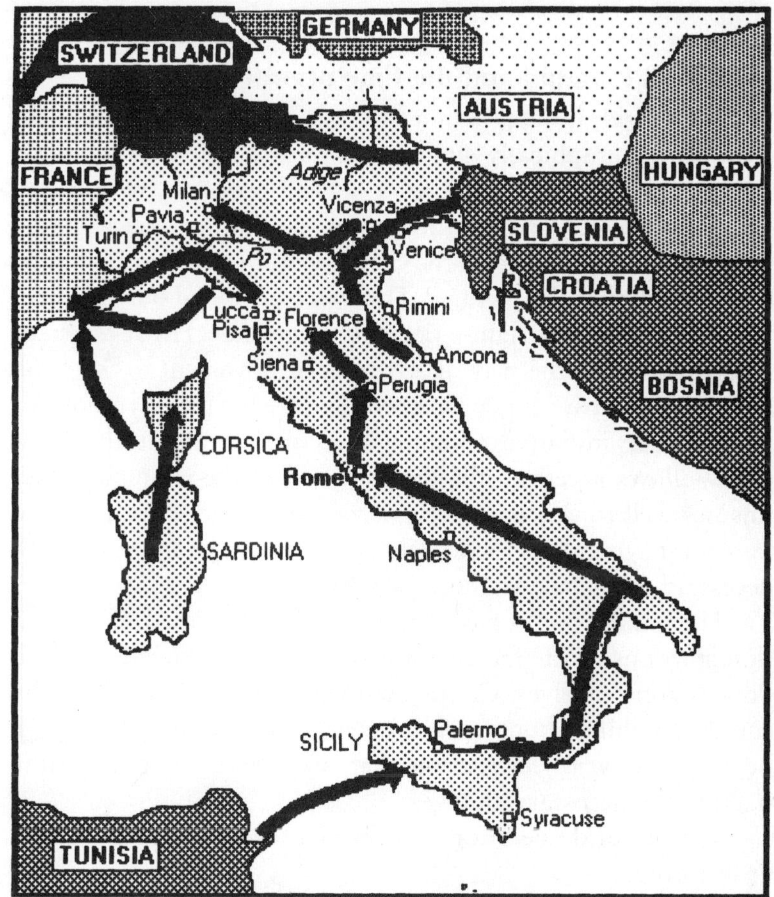

The invasion and fall of Italy

to Florence, from Venice to Turin. Within Italy itself, all kinds of atrocities are starting to be committed under the new occupation regime. Throughout the continent economies and alliances are rapidly collapsing, while national rearmament is proceeding apace. Possibly the financial effects are spreading to America and the Far East, too. Certainly the contours of the **Great Pyramid**'s Subterranean Chamber seem to foreshadow some such world-wide crisis for the period in question (see the diagram overleaf).

The Great Pyramid and the time of ordeal

The world, in fact, is in a mess, and it is this mess that the chamber so graphically symbolises, as explained on page 12. Broadly, the picture is of a kind of 'hell on earth' with a bottomless pit directly facing those who, as they symbolically pass through time, would cross the chamber from north to south (i.e. from the right of the picture). This can be avoided only by making a detour to their right—i.e. their 'good' side. However, steep rock ridges lie in the way of any further movement to the right, and only a narrow gulley roughly opposite the pit—symbolising a reforming initiative of some difficulty at about the same date—allows access to the far west end of the chamber. Since this lies well to the west of the Pyramid's centre-line, arrival at this point symbolises in turn the achievement of more than the necessary inner balance necessary for salvation.

The implication is more or less as already hinted. If destruction stares us in the face, then it is because we have brought it down upon ourselves. Consequently it is we, and only we, who can do anything about it. And indeed, it is the immediate prospect of that very destruction that may serve to spur us into making the necessary changes.

It is out of desperation, in other words, that true hope may at last arise.

The chamber spells out the likely developments in detail. Entered (symbolically at least) in around the year 1914, it brings those entering it (i.e. errant humanity) to the deepest part of the pit in its floor in around 2003—though in both cases there appears to be a built-in tolerance of ±3 years or so[11]—and the first of the equally-symbolic 'steps' leading out of it to the south does not occur until around 2055. There is, in other words, a rock-bottom crisis of about fifty-two years.

That crisis is essentially a material one. We should expect the basic structures that underlie our whole civilisation to suffer severe damage. Our financial structures, our communications networks, our supplies of raw-materials and consequently our

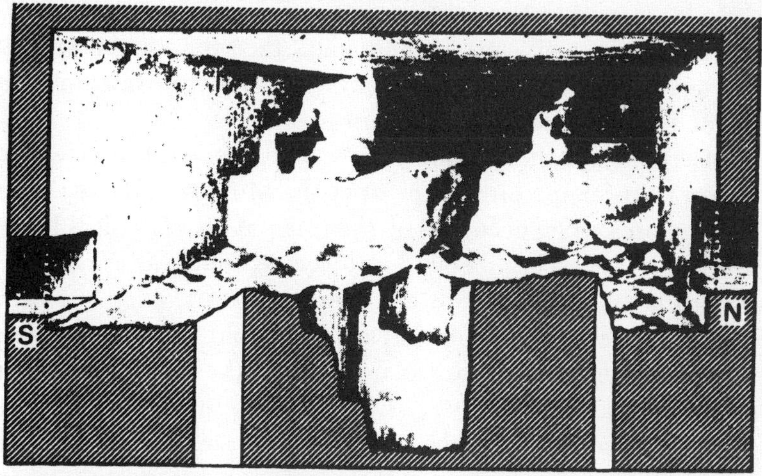

The Great Pyramid's Great Subterranean Chamber[12] (movement from right (N) to left (S) signifies humanity's progress through time)

whole standard of living are at severe risk. For some decades we may be forced back into a much more primitive way of life characterised by self-sufficiency and closeness to the land. Especially during the change-over, social unrest, conflict and disintegration may result.

Which might argue (as **Edgar Cayce** did) for getting a good deal closer to the land in the first place.

As we shall see, this fits the events foreseen by **Nostradamus** with some accuracy. With the Church in turmoil, southern Europe in deep financial trouble as it falls to the invaders, and the countries of the eastern Mediterranean not only under brutal enemy occupation but devastated by earthquakes and tidal waves as well, the period is clearly destined to be a time of catastrophic crisis.

But does this apply to the world as a whole?

Rather like the **Bible, Nostradamus** is prone to make what are often merely local or regional events look suspiciously like universal ones—and much the same may apply to the **Great Pyramid,** too. When the biblical prophets foresaw the world falling about their ears, that world was in all probability merely their *local* world. And when, similarly, the **Great Pyramid** appears to predict disaster for humanity, then that disaster could just as conceivably be merely *local* humanity—the humanity of Egypt and the Middle East generally.

Certainly, if the predictions are to be believed, that whole region is in for the direst time of crisis. Moreover, having been the first area to be occupied by the oriental invaders, it is likely to be the last to be liberated—always assuming that that liberation is set to come (if at all) from the West.

Yet, especially in today's world of rapid communications, it is no longer possible to isolate areas of the world from each other in quite the same way as it once was. In economic circles it is sometimes said that when America sneezes, Europe catches a cold. But the reverse is possibly increasingly true as well: when Europe suffers a stroke, America falls flat on its face. And so, possibly, does the rest of the world's economic community as well.

Communication, in other words, produces community. As John Donne so memorably put it over two hundred years ago: 'No man is an island, entire of itself.'

Thus it is, then, that just as Europe's wars nowadays soon tend to become World Wars, so Europe's coming crisis, too, may quickly become a world crisis—and one of almost unprecedented severity, at that. Yet even in this there may be some hope. For the deeper America and the rest of the world are sucked in, the more likely is it that they will eventually become involved in the extrication process, too. Not for the first time, in other words, American forces may eventually—and however reluctantly—be impelled by sheer self-interest to step in and help save Europe from itself.

Chapter and verse

It is, after all, largely as a result of a mixture of European apathy, inertia and incompetence that the invaders will have been allowed to overrun the Balkans in the first place. So, at least, **Nostradamus** constantly suggests in respect of the invasion as a whole. By way of popular reaction to this, however, there seems to be a brief bout of wild war-fever, if *Century* XII.55 applies at this point. Traitors and fleecers, it reveals, are busy bamboozling governments themselves into taking up unwise warlike policies. Eventually, however, calmer counsels prevail—indeed, there is a swing to the opposite extreme—and *Century* II.39 sees what appears to be the European Union falling prey to fatal complacency (see p. 63).

But then French, Germans and Spaniards alike (warns Nostradamus in the same verse) will always have been dangerously over-confident—and they will still be so only a year before the invaders finally strike in the year 2000. It will take the catastrophic collapse of what, in the original, he calls their 'schoolhouse republic' to bring them back down to earth again.

By and large, in fact, the peoples of the Western democracies will be far more interested in carrying on with their hedonistic lifestyles than in taking the oriental threat seriously. The consequences will be disastrous. Even while they are still in the midst of a constant round of public entertainments, ritual celebrations and general beanfeasts to celebrate the Millennium, Mesopotamian (i.e. Iraqi) forces will suddenly descend on them, and before they know where they are, southern Italy will be invaded, Rome taken and the Pope already fled to France (VII. 22).

Whether in Sicily, Italy or eventually France (Nostradamus continues at I.11), it will be the same old story over and over again. 'Addled idiocy' at the top will be directly responsible for bringing down war and all its horrors on the people's heads. Not that the brutal invaders will be without plenty of their own responsibility for what happens, of course. But wise decisions—whether political, military or even philosophical—could so easily avert the coming threat if taken early enough.

Unfortunately, however, such wisdom is far from universal among politicians. The short-term nature of most of their appointments too easily encourages political short-sightedness, and the personal enjoyment of power (and especially the boost that it can give to one's own dogmas and illusions) is so much more enticing than exercising it for the genuine public good.

The upshot is likely to be all too familiar. As crisis looms and the invaders appear on the horizon in ever greater numbers, all that the politicians will manage to do will be to hold endless conferences and sign dubious agreements that will merely make matters worse. Nostradamus sums it all up in the single, pregnant first line of *Présage* 83:

Leaders hold talks while Christendom is shaken;
By alien hordes the Holy Seat's attacked.
Their advent first as ill, then lethal taken,
From th' east death, plague, famine and evil pact.

As a result, what was originally merely a threat quickly develops into a major catastrophe. The Vatican is stormed, and Death, ably assisted by half-hearted alliances and valueless pacts, is allowed to march into Western Europe followed by all his usual train of grisly attendants—the dreaded Plague among them.

The return of the Plague

Whether **Nostradamus** actually *means* Plague at this point is not entirely clear. Certainly he refers to it again and again in the context of the spreading conflict. As a doctor who himself specialised in treating the disease, he presumably knew what he was talking about. And indeed, renewed Plague epidemics in our own era are by no means out of the question. Contrary to popular supposition, the ancient disease did not just disappear with the advent of sanitation, improved hygiene and modern medicine. It still flourishes in the shellfish of our estuarial waters, as well as on land in whole populations of wild rodents. To most of these latter—whether in Asia or on the west coast of America—it is not lethal. But when it spreads to more vulnerable species all hell can be let loose, as they die off and their infected fleas seek refuge amid the welcoming hairs of other passing creatures. For man is one of those creatures, and to him it can prove absolutely devastating. In the Middle Ages, after all, it successfully wiped out up to a third of the population of Europe—and it has to be said that Nostradamus's subsequent descriptions of the future epidemic's after-effects read uncomfortably like a re-run of those of the former Black Death.

Once again, consequently, we are reminded of the **Bible**'s prophecies in this regard. '*Lo, it is coming: disaster upon disaster . . . your doom is upon you . . . The sword without, pestilence and famine within*', warns the prophet **Ezekiel** at 7:5, 7, 15. The *Revelation of John*, similarly, couples pestilence with war: the 'seven bowls of the wrath of God' that are poured out upon errant humanity in chapter 16 contain not just a whole variety of plagues, including 'foul, malignant sores', *but Armageddon itself.*

And the sixth bowlful, be it noted, has the specific effect of drying up the river Euphrates to open up the way for the dreaded 'kings from the East'.

Edgar Cayce enthusiasts will also be gratified to learn that the seventh bowl produces '*an earthquake stronger than any ever seen before in history*', while mountains are levelled and islands vanish.

All this is for the future, however. The main concern for the Europeans of the early 2000s will be with the immediate military invasion. Or rather, it ought to be. And yet reality still seems likely to be extraordinarily slow to sink in, if *Century* VIII.72 is to be believed. Even with Rome already in the invaders' hands, the Italians in particular will be unwilling to fight, and much too concerned with enjoying their usual family comforts. Declining to give battle on what is apparently a public holiday, they will (as already foreshadowed) suffer a huge defeat at Perugia, followed by another in the area of Ravenna. And meanwhile the countryside all around will be ravaged (as war-torn countrysides are wont to be) by foraging hordes of ill-fed enemy troops.

For, as **Mario de Sabato** has already hinted, these will be largely devoid of equipment or supplies, and therefore forced to forage for everything they need.

The rape of France

It is at this point, it seems, that the victorious invaders start to turn their eyes towards France. As **Nostradamus** puts it at *Sixain* 44, once again using his liturgical count:

The beauteous rose that all in France admire
A mighty Prince shall in the end desire:
Six hundred ten shall see his passion rise.
After five years herself she'll wounded find
By Cupid's dart, and in his arms entwined
If fifteen see him aided from the skies.

The terms are highly allegorical, but the underlying message is brutally clear. There is to be a long campaign against the French—a virtual rape, in fact, for Cupid/Eros was always the god of lust rather than love—which will start in 2002 and increase in ferocity until 2007, finally overpowering the country when aerial attacks are added to the equation in 2017.

Moreover, the insidious disease of procrastination and inaction that has so paralysed Italy is now set to spread to France, too. As a result, with the area around Siena in Italy already awash with blood, the invaders—temporarily baulked in their attempt to advance along the Mediterranean coast between the Alps and the sea—are allowed to mount a ferocious sea-borne attack on Marseille instead. And once again it is the same old story, as *Centuries* I.18 and III.79 reveal. While the generals and politicians are arguing amongst themselves, and the defences are consequently allowed to go to rack and ruin, Muslim naval forces are permitted to enter the port of Marseille virtually unopposed.

So it is, then, that the alien regime gains its first foothold in France, and the hordes of invaders, as Nostradamus graphically puts it, are soon as thick as flies. Indeed, the only positive outcome—if there is one—is that French resolve and resistance at last start to stiffen, too late though this may now prove to be. As *Sixain* 23 puts it, with its naval metaphor and its liturgical dating of 1999 or 2002:

When the great ship of state, from stem to stern,
Of France and all things that its life concern,
With rocks and waves is shattered by the sea,
Its heart assailed, the ebb with corpses strewed—
Yet by this ill its life shall be renewed.
Six hundred seven or ten these things shall be.

Cry 'Havoc!' and let slip the dogs of war

The ensuing chain of events was first decoded and spelt out in my earlier translation *Nostradamus—The Next 50 Years*. And the upshot is a sobering one.

Having successfully established their beach-head, the invaders soon overrun the whole of Provence, then advance up the Rhône valley to Lyon (which **Nostradamus**, punning astrologically on its name, refers to as the 'solar city'), as well as descending on the city from the Alpine passes to the east. As *Century* V.81 reveals, the siege is destined to last seven months. Overhead, a premonitory bird proclaims doom on the inhabitants each night (Nostradamus appears to associate it with the 'eagle of doom' of St John's Revelation, whose characteristic call of 'Oee! Oee!' he actually reproduces as 'Huy! Huy!' in his accompanying letter to his patron, the French King Henri II—but the creature may in reality be some kind of loudspeaker aircraft engaged in psychological warfare). Then the assault from the east resumes in earnest, and within a week the invaders have entered the city.

The account continues at VIII.6 and III.7. Lyon duly falls, its destruction marked by a huge glare that could be either a massive firestorm or a nuclear attack. Bombarded by swarms

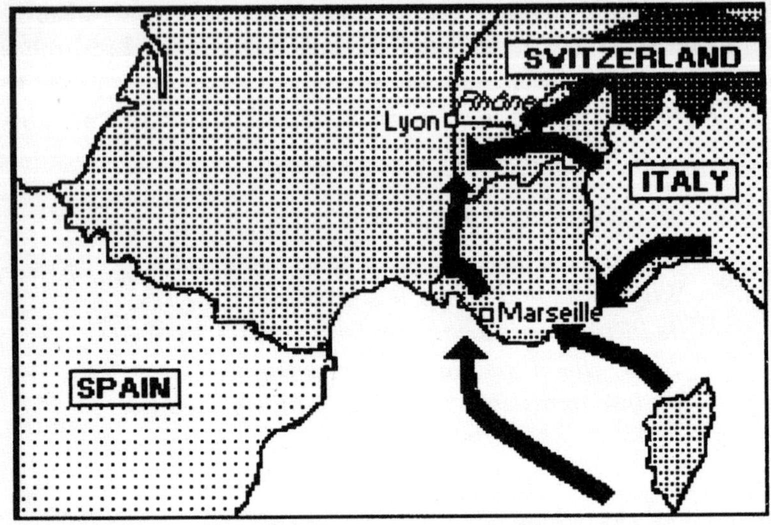

The Muslim assault on Provence

of wheeling aircraft that Nostradamus likens to fighting crows, the citizens flee for their lives, And meanwhile Malta, too, has fallen, the French authorities in the south of France are trying to do deals with the 'Moors'—which may suggest that the North African Muslims, too, are already posing a growing threat of their own—and the Swiss are plotting defence-strategies with the British, while still putting it about that they propose to remain neutral in the conflict.

Only in central and eastern Europe—and especially in Hungary—are the Asiatic hordes likely to be met with much in the way of firm and resolute resistance. As they push steadily northwards from Serbia, valiant Hungarian military efforts (not helped, as X.61 and II.24 reveal, by internal plots to hand over the country lock, stock and barrel to the enemy, still less by reluctance on the part of the rest of the new eastern Europe to come to its assistance) succeed in keeping them to the south and west of the Danube—even though this necessarily means that the twin capital cities of Buda and Pest finish up split between the two sides (X.62, II.90):

From Serbia he'll Hungary attack,
Though Buda's envoy try him to divert:
The Turkish chief, Slavonia at his back
To Arab law would Hungary convert.

A life-death fight, a changing of regimes
Bring laws more stern than abject servitude.
Hungary shall be full of cries and screams
When for dominion its twin cities feud.

The dire upshot

The results for Italy—as for Greece—are already catastrophic, as **Nostradamus**'s prediction for the first week of May 2002 reveals (*Century* I.83). The invaders are in full control, sharing out all the booty that was at least part of their original motivation. By the following year, consequently, their leaders are sufficiently sure of themselves to meet near Venice to plan phase two of their operation (IV.68).

And meanwhile the Western economies are in trouble. As the astrology of *Century* II.65 could well suggest, by December of 2004 not merely northern Italy, but the West generally, are rapidly descending into almost terminal financial crisis. And the crisis is not only financial. Large parts of Europe's population are already enduring once again the slavery of enemy occupation, while the Church, with its buildings in flames and its faithful persecuted by the claimed representatives of Islam, is virtually on its last legs.

The **Great Pyramid**'s apparent prediction of a long period of material crisis, then, seems more than amply justified.

Bad news for the Vatican

Not surprisingly, therefore, the papacy is in crisis, too. Using his 'ecclesiastical count' to refer to the beginning of the year 2001, **Nostradamus** has already described the election of the current Pope's successor (X.91). An Italian from the southern region of Campania who is somehow characterised by the colours black and grey, he will turn out gravely to disappoint the Church's hopes. '*Never worse fiend; never more grave mistake!*' warns the seer cryptically.

This figure is presumably the next on **St Malachy**'s list—namely *Gloria Olivae*, or 'Glory of the Olive'. Traditionally, the expression is interpreted as indicating a peaceful reign, while I myself have in the past suggested the possibility of a black Pope.[8] But in view of **Nostradamus**'s other revelations, and **St Malachy**'s earlier misleading reference to *Aquila Rapax* (see p. 23), another interpretation suggests itself: the 'glory of the olive' in fact refers to the baleful triumph of the olive-skinned races that are now sweeping across southern Europe from the Middle East.

As for the new Pope himself, he is severely criticised on all sides, and is consequently replaced almost before his reign has begun. The elections for his successor, whom (as we saw earlier) **St Malachy** names *Petrus II Romanus* ('Peter the Second of Rome'), are deliberately rigged—if admittedly under brutal duress on the part of the invaders—and the last pontiff of the present series then proceeds to betray the Church by allowing the aliens' wishes to override Vatican policy in exchange for the Holy See's continued survival.

If so, it will not be the first time that this has happened—not, at least, if we are to believe those who criticise Pope Pius XII for allegedly soft-pedalling his criticisms of the occupying Germans' persecution of the Jews during the Second World War.

But that is not the end of it. Rome itself is now destroyed by fire (*Century* II.93), while the new Pope is imprisoned in some kind of underground dungeon not far from the Tiber. Here we are once again reminded, then, of **St Malachy**'s dramatic final prophecy concerning him, '*During the final persecution of the Holy Roman Church shall reign Peter II of Rome, who shall feed his sheep amidst many tribulations and, by the*

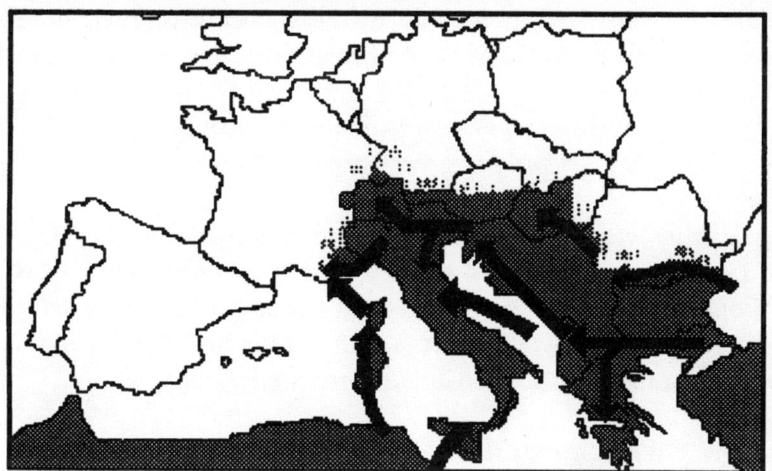

The Muslim advance: progress up to 2005

time these are over, the City of the Seven Hills shall be destroyed and the terrible Judge shall judge his people.'

In *Sixain* 42, 'liturgically' dated for 2002, **Nostradamus** (punning outrageously—but, it has to be said, entirely typically—on the city's name) likewise identifies a Rome in a state of dire unrest, and surrounded by marauding bands of combatants:

That mighty Town where roams the first of men
(I've named the place—just read the line again)
Is sore alarmed, with soldiers all afield.
Both war and flood the City shall assail
Till rescuing Frenchmen shall once more prevail.
Six hundred ten: then see these things revealed.

Unsurprisingly, perhaps (in the light of the **Bible**'s *Revelation of John*), **St Ambrose,** like **St Malachy**, coupled the eventual fall of Rome with the coming of the Antichrist, and saw them both as signs of the Last Days, while the **Venerable Bartolomeo di**

Saluzzo, who lived at the end of the sixteenth century, is reported as prophesying of Rome's final days:

Like bull shall bellow Moorish Turk:
In iron and fire great harm shall lurk.

As if this were not enough, the **Venerable Bede**, too (c. 673–735), left us a celebrated prophecy on the subject. This reads: '*Coliseum stabit et Roma. Quando cadet Coliseum, cadet et Roma: quando cadet Roma, cadet et mundus.*' Or, as Byron was to translate it in his *Childe Harold's Pilgrimage:*

While stands the Coliseum, Rome shall stand;
When falls the Coliseum, Rome shall fall;
And when Rome falls—the World.

Mother earth joins in

But there is worse to come. During August 2004 (if **Nostradamus** is to be believed) the whole of the eastern Mediterranean is due to be rocked by huge earthquakes (*Centuries* II.52, III.3). The similarity to the **Bible**'s end-time scenario seems more than a little disturbing. Marked by a conjunction of Mercury, Mars and the moon, these will centre on central Turkey, with Ephesus and Corinth particularly hard hit, and will be accompanied by the onset of a period of southern drought.

More to the point, however, they will give rise to enormous tidal waves. These will go on to devastate many Mediterranean countries (VIII.16, I.69). Greece in particular will be overwhelmed, with waves even mounting the flanks of Mount Olympus. *Century* V.31 suggests that virtually the whole of its lowland culture will be wiped out, its ancient monuments laid in even more abject ruins than before. (This seems to be broadly in line with **Edgar Cayce**'s prediction for 1998 or 2000, if a few years late in date.)

Meanwhile, not the least of the countries affected will of

course be Italy itself, as V.63 reveals. As if its existing woes of famine, plague, occupation and bloody persecution were not enough, widespread flooding will now take place, with boats having to be used to rescue survivors. A little later, indeed, Britain will also be flooded (IX.31, III.70)—though possibly this has more to do with **Edgar Cayce**'s inundations than with **Nostradamus**'s Mediterranean earthquakes.

Pause for breath

Following all these calamities, though, the year 2005 at least marks a temporary pause in the Muslim onslaught. Evidently the invaders have decided to take time for recuperation and reinforcement, using Italy as their prime base in Europe. No doubt, too, they have been set back by all the natural upheavals, just like everybody else. **Nostradamus**'s *Présage* 8 seems to pinpoint Florence as a centre of temporary rest and healing for the occupying forces—and possibly as a regional military headquarters, too.

At present, it seems, the Muslims are not inclined to advance much further into France than Lyon and the Rhône valley. Possibly their forces have become over-stretched and over-tired. Almost certainly, too, French resistance has stiffened and been made much more watertight. It is the southern wing of the advance, still sweeping across North Africa, that now has France and the Iberian peninsula in its sights. But here much depends on just how long the Western navies can maintain control of the western Mediterranean.

Subsequent sections will, as we shall see, duly answer that question.

But in the meantime there will be a chance for the West to reorganise, to make policy, to get its priorities straight. There will be deep questions to be answered—not just of military strategy, but of underlying purpose. Is self-defence always justified, even in the face of overwhelming odds? Is there such a thing as a Holy War? Can brutality successfully be met with brutality? Are fatalism or appeasement ever justified? Have we deserved everything we get?

What, in short, is wise, and what is just? And before trying to set the world to rights, might we not first need to set *ourselves* to rights?

Or is the one merely another aspect of the other, and so capable of being dealt with at one and the same time?

2006–2010

• DATE SUMMARY •

Arrows indicate the beginning ↓ and end ↑ of a prophetic window

2006	Feb	Local Italian leader murdered at Fossano on orders from Rome (*Nostradamus*)
	↕	World-library established (*Arthur C. Clarke*)
	↕	Sea-bed mining begins (*Arthur C. Clarke*)
2007	↑	End of window for start of era of destruction and/or total collapse of materialist civilisation (*Great Pyramid*)
	May(?)↓	Beginning of two-year window for birth of Henri V, future King of France and most of Europe (*Nostradamus*)
	Sept	Western navies abandon Mediterranean: Asiatic invasion resumes via North Africa (*Nostradamus*)
	↓	France under renewed attack (*Nostradamus*)

2007	↓	Death of France begins (*Nostradamus*)
2008		No specific events predicted
2009		Anti-French violence by Muslim Arabs reaches peak (*Nostradamus*)
2010		Earliest *astronomical* date for start of Age of Aquarius (*Institut Géographique National*)

•COMMENTARY•

TRUE IT MAY BE THAT THE **GREAT PYRAMID**'S MAIN SUBTERRANEAN chamber marks out the year 2007 as the last likely date for the start of the period of 'hell on earth' that it symbolises. But then, if **Nostradamus** is to be believed, that period will long since have got under way in any case.

For a while, admittedly, there is something of a stalemate in the oriental campaign against Europe, on the ground at least. Nostradamus mentions little specifically for 2006 or 2007 apart from the murder on 13 February 2006 of a local leader at Fossano on the orders of the new regime in Rome (*Century* III.96).

The battle for the high seas

Perhaps this is because the main action has now moved to the high seas. For the next major encounter reported by **Nostradamus** is a huge naval battle in the course of which the sea will actually become red with blood. He refers to the occasion not merely in his prose writings, but at *Centuries* IX.42, I.37, IX.100, II.78, III.1 and II.85, the last of which seems to link it in time with the eventual fall of Lyon.

This would suggest, then, that it will take place very near the beginning of the period under discussion, probably in 2006, or even during the preceding year. Nostradamus's descriptions of it are graphic. The initial clash takes place shortly before sunset, somewhere between Marseille and Tunis (I.37, IX.100). There are hints of the use of thermal and chemical weapons, and by nightfall the Western fleets are already on their way to the bottom, their flagship either captured or awash with human blood.

The Western naval force seems to be an international one, but the French obstinately decline to send reinforcements to rectify the situation, while the British, who are also supposed to be taking part, deliberately take steps to ensure that their submarines arrive late, so sabotaging the entire defence-strategy for what appear to be crass political reasons (II.78). As a result, when they do at last arrive they find a sea already red with the blood of both sides. For Nostradamus the picture evidently looms vividly enough in his nightly visions for him to return to it repeatedly: it almost has the character of a recurrent dream.

Blame for the incident—which now leaves all the Mediterranean islands wide open to enemy invasion—falls on the local British commander, but in the light of their own culpability in the matter, as well as in the face of the growing threat, the French authorities are not inclined to make too much of it, lest the British withdraw altogether (VI.90). '*Stinking, outrageous, and a rank disgrace*,' the prophet calls it. Some members of the French fleet obviously agree, staging what amounts to a mutiny (VII.37)—but their attempts to find and lynch the British admiral come to nothing, largely because he has had the foresight to stay safely ashore at La Nerthe, just to the north-west of Marseille.

This is an interesting detail, indicating as it does that at the time Marseille itself has not yet fallen. The fact that Nostradamus also links the subsequent fall of Malta with that of Lyon would suggest a date of around 2005 for this whole complex of events. It is their massive naval victory, in other words, that actually makes it possible for the invaders to attack Marseille in the first place: and it is this in turn that leads to the overrunning of Provence and in due course to the catastrophic fall of Lyon.

With the French navy in particular almost annihilated, the British are now virtually cock of the naval roost—on the Western side, at least. But neither this nor their apparent new-made threat to use both Polaris and Trident nuclear weapons succeeds in deterring the invaders (III.1). Despite further naval battles, in which guided missiles seem to be involved (II.40), Muslim sea-power merely grows and spreads.

The invasion from Africa

Soon, consequently, Muslims from North Africa are not only raiding the French Riviera, but invading the Balearic islands and even crossing into Europe via the Straits of Gibraltar. V.11 suggests (if somewhat obtusely) an astrological date of September 2007 for this general development, while both *Sixain* 44 (see p. 86) and *Sixain* 54 (p. 113) also appear to tie the start of the 'death of France' to the 'liturgical' year '615—i.e. 2007.

Nostradamus describes the new sea-borne invasion vividly, at the same time looking ahead to the time when it will eventually reach Pamplona, in the Pyrenean foothills (*Sixain* 41):

Vessels and ships, their banners flying high,
Near Cape Gibraltar shall the issue try,
And on Pamplona grievous crimes descend.
A thousand deadly woes the place shall rack,
Full many a time the subject of attack,
Yet to the Empire falling in the end.

The seer likens the invasion (*Century* II.30) to that of the Carthaginian (i.e. Tunisian) general Hannibal in classical times, thus giving a broad indication of the new invasion's route, too. At VI.80 he confirms it: the invaders are due to flood into Europe from Morocco via Gibraltar, spreading almost universal death and destruction in their wake. Thanks once again partly to treachery and incompetence among the defenders, as III.20 reveals, the forces of Islam will succeed in driving the Spanish

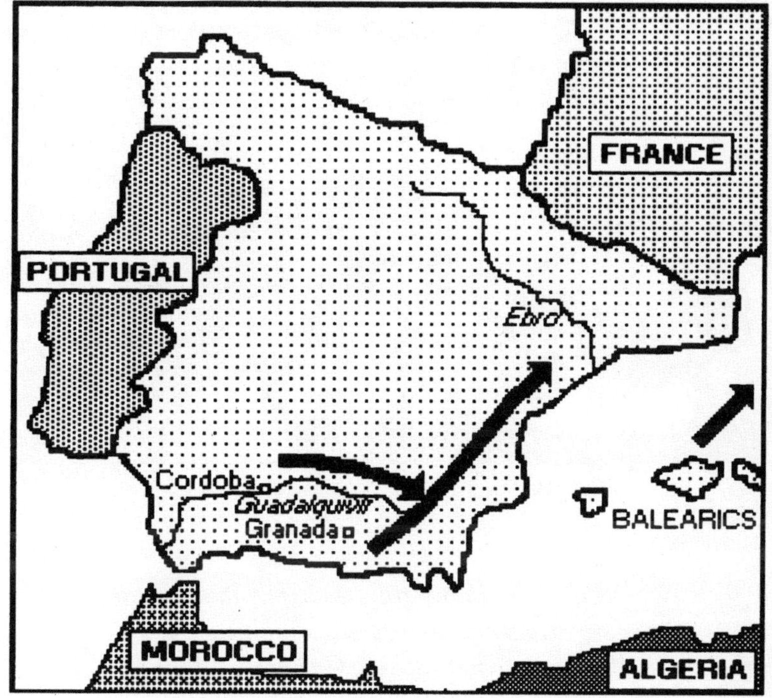

The invasion of Spain

before them, ruthlessly ‘cleansing’ the land of Christians all the way from Cordoba and Granada in the south to the river Ebro in the east.

Century X.48 depicts the developing invasion in the most striking of terms:

> *Marching from deepest Spain their banners see!*
> *From Europe’s furthest borders press their steeds.*
> *Troubles they’ll have crossing the narrow sea:*
> *Guerilla war their mighty host impedes.*

So it is that Western Europe (and France particularly) is due to be faced with even further disasters that are largely of its own making. In *Présages* 29 and 11 **Nostradamus** chronicles the gathering storm for his countrymen with frightening vividness:

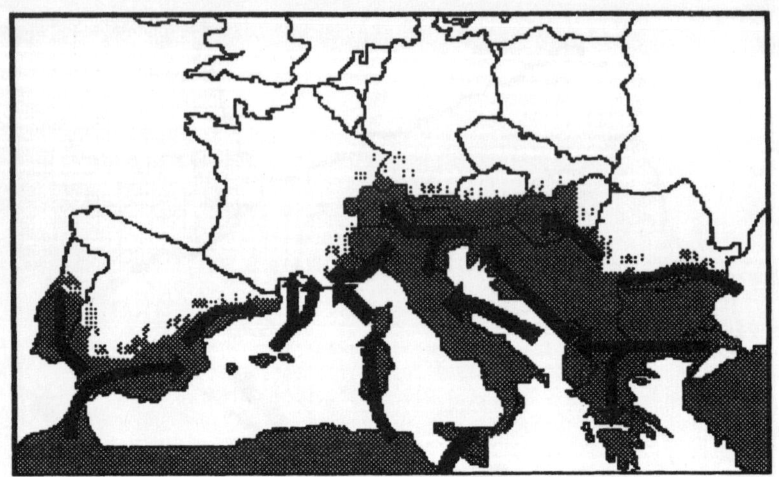

The Muslim invasion: progress up to 2010

War thunders. Many folk their farmlands quit.
Borders attacked, terrors and rumours fly.
Chief betrays chief. Spain, Germany admit
The refugees. The Muslim fleet draws nigh.

The sight of it shall make the sky to weep.
Hannibal lays his plans. War fleets prepare.
St Denis pours. The ships delay, nor keep
Silent of what they know not, nor you care.

Here there seems to be some suggestion not merely of rain, but of further chemical or biological warfare (*Présage* 125 refers specifically to a 'mess of oily stains' afflicting the fruit-trees), while the apparent reference to the feast of St Denis may suggest a date of 9 October. The last two lines of the second verse seem to refer once again to the naval disaster already described—though it has to be said that the original phrasing is particularly obtuse at this point.

A place for optimism?

In the light of all this, one naturally starts to wonder what place there could possibly be in the general scheme of things for the scientific advances tentatively predicted by **Arthur C. Clarke** for the period in question (see the date summary at the beginning of this chapter), let alone for the much more dramatic ones supposedly already embarked upon a decade or so earlier. Enterprises such as exploring the planets and developing remote energy-transmission, after all, cost money. Fortunately, though, the establishment of a world-library is likely to happen largely of its own accord, thanks to the development of international computer networks, while mining the sea-bed is likely—after high initial costs—to be greatly to the benefit of those involved in it.

There is just a chance, then, that these may indeed occur on time. Yet the developing situation in Europe—to say nothing of **Edgar Cayce**'s predicted geological upheavals in America and the Far East—could yet put a spanner in the works, for the time being at least.

But then, possibly the truth is that **Clarke**'s visions were originally predicated on the basis of 'all things being equal'. They are extrapolations, in other words, based (as all extrapolations naturally have to be) on present circumstances and on the assumption that the underlying trends will continue relatively undisturbed into the future.

Unfortunately, however, the signs are that all things will not be equal. The underlying trends will not continue undisturbed—other, that is, than the underlying human tendency to murder, rape and pillage whenever the thin veneer of civilisation breaks down, as it so easily can. Clarke himself admits that social disruption could yet spell doom for his predictions.

Consequently the only real ray of light to pierce the gloom of this particularly dark period is **Nostradamus**'s vision of the birth of a future leader from the ancient royal line of France, who will eventually help to impose a new order on a new Europe, once the invaders have at long last been expelled . . .

The Age of Aquarius

What, then, of the much-vaunted Age of Aquarius, which according to the French Institut Géographique National is due to commence—astronomically at least—in 2010, when the vernal equinox enters the constellation of the Water-Carrier? The symbolism of **aeonic astrology**[10] would suggest that this should be not only a watery time, but also an era during which the imprisoned fishes of the Age of Pisces—imprisoned, that is, to the extent that they are bound to each other, presumably by the unforgiving law of Karma—are finally released. Poured out of the celestial pitcher of Aquarius into the infinite ocean of the cosmos, they are then freed to pursue their individual destinies, unshackled by petty animosities, major hatreds or fundamental divisions—unshackled, in short, by the perpetual 'tit for tat' of self-imposed duality, where everything has to be seen in terms of good and bad, right and wrong, light and dark, accepted and rejected. The biblical 'Fall', you will recall, occurred when man and woman first started to eat the fruit of the Tree of the Knowledge of Good and Evil; and the biblical Redemption will presumably occur when they finally stop.

On the other hand, there is another aspect of duality which will presumably have to disappear at exactly the same time—and it is the basic duality which underlies all of the above. This is the distinction not merely between 'I' and 'you', but even between 'I' and 'me'—all of it due to be washed away, like so much else, by the waters of Aquarius.

Human beings, in other words, are not only going to have to stop imagining that they are somehow distinct and separate from everybody else, inhabitants of a totally interconnected universe who can nevertheless somehow stand outside it and subject it to their will. They are also going to have to resolve the perpetual inner conflict between spirit and matter, between mind and body, between conscious and unconscious, between thought and feeling. Outer war and inner war alike are going to have to cease.

Or rather they simply *will* cease—for there is no question of somehow imposing such an outcome upon ourselves by act of will, which would merely be yet another manifestation of the self-same inner conflict. It will happen, in other words, simply because the time is right. The *Zeitgeist* of the Age of Aquarius will have claimed its due.

It will be an idea whose time has come. And nothing, as Victor Hugo realised, is more powerful.

And so all warfare will cease. The swords, as the **Bible** puts it, will be beaten into ploughshares, the spears into pruning-hooks. Everybody will sit at peace under their vines. And God will wipe away all tears from their eyes.

It is not generally realised that the self-same outcome is foreseen by **aeonic astrology**, too. For the celestial figure of Aquarius is not alone. Beneath him swims yet another fish—the enormous sea-creature known as *Piscis Australis*, or the 'Southern Fish'. True, it swims, for the most part, just below the southern horizon—or only marginally above it—and so is normally invisible to northern Europeans. But its function is a truly vital one. Its task is to swallow up all the fishes newly released from Aquarius's pitcher. Not in any predatory sense, though. The point is simply the old one that 'you are what you eat'. The myriad separate fishes of the Age of Pisces swim willingly into the jaws of the greater fish of Aquarius. Their bodies become its body, their minds its mind, their consciousness its consciousness.

In this distinctly watery age, in other words, humanity at last becomes one—a myriad fishy souls in search of a single, common destiny.

No wonder that, after all the potential horrors of the interim, peace seems destined to break out at long last. No wonder, too, that the biblical prophet **Joel**'s prophecy of a time when '*your sons and your daughters shall prophesy, your old men shall dream dreams, and your young men shall see visions*' seems to be starting to come true even in our own day. Already the psychic doors are opening, just as all across the Elysian prairies of cyberspace new, 'virtual' realities are dawning and the divisions between minds all over the world are at last promising to break down.

The individual inhabitants of earth have already set out on the long path that will turn them into the eventual ten thousand million or so brain-cells of a much greater, collective human consciousness. Whether we realise it or not, we have already committed ourselves, as we converge upon what **Teilhard de Chardin** called *Omega Point*, to becoming members of that greater body which **St Paul** identified with the future Cosmic Christ himself—the Second Adam, the *Adam Kadmon* or Archetypal Man long ago envisioned by the ancient Pharisees.

The *Logos*. The Word. The Hindus' *Purusha*. Man-as-in-the-mind-of-God.[8,9]

With the dawning of the Age of Aquarius, the fishes will finally become fish, humans finally human, Christians finally Christ.

Jesus, too, seems to have foreseen that outcome. The one who will lead the disciples to the Upper Room of the Passover—symbolic of the great Messianic Banquet that will be spread for the redeemed in the Promised Land of the Kingdom of Heaven on earth—is to be 'a man carrying a pitcher of water': *Aquarius, in other words*. And the only sign that Jesus promised them was 'the sign of the prophet Jonah'—the man whose chief claim to fame is of course that he was *eaten by a mighty fish*.

A word of caution

But there is a snag. The transition from celestial age to celestial age tends to be a disturbed one. The gospels have the disciples spending a stormy night at sea before calm returns with the dawn and the breakfast of fishes is finally laid out in the presence of the Messiah on the shore of eternity.

Tradition has it that this time of troubles normally lasts some fifty years. For some twenty-five years either side of the cusp, in other words, chaos may well break loose—just the sort of mayhem, in fact, that **Nostradamus** and the other prophets have been describing all along.

Which means that it may well be at least 2035 before the Age of Aquarius can dawn in all its glory and **Nostradamus**'s European saviour can finally take up his role.

But then this is purely from the astronomical viewpoint. In strictly *astrological* terms, the vernal sun does not enter the *sign* of Aquarius until around 2375. Indeed, in terms of *tropical* (i.e. traditional) astrology, it never enters it at all, since at the spring equinox (20/21 March) the sun is always presumed to be *at the first point of Aries.*

The message is clear: *tradition is the obstacle*. All things, as the **Bible** has it, have to be made new. And if it is really electronics that is destined finally to open the doors to global consciousness—and not merely, as a good many 'spiritual' people insist, some kind of inner transformation—then *everybody* will need access to it, including the Third World. No wonder there has to be a time of turbulence and a vast reallocation of resources.

Inner transformation may come—but outer transformation will have to precede it.

It ill behoves us to imagine, then (as a good many old-fashioned New Agers are all too prone to do) that any day now the Kingdom of Heaven will somehow fall like some ready-ripened fruit into our laps, if only we can keep the vision clear, stay positive and avoid thinking about all the nasty things that might stand between us and it.

'Negativity' isn't the problem. *We* are the problem.

We are the ones who insist on behaving like children. *We* are the ones who want to eat our cake and have it too. In fact we have already long since eaten that cake—or, if you prefer the pseudo-biblical image, that apple. But having eaten it, we now have no choice but to pay for it. That is the only way in which we can possibly have another bite.

To put it in perfectly clear and down-to-earth terms, we in the so-called First World especially have already made free with

The constellation of Aquarius, complete with Piscis Australis[10]

the rest of the world for our own exclusive benefit. We have collared its resources and enslaved its peoples (whether institutionally or merely economically). In every conceivable way—racially, culturally, spiritually, psychologically, medically, financially, industrially—we have for centuries insisted (to use a crude but wonderfully revealing expression) on laying all our shit on them. But if **Nostradamus** and the other prophets teach us nothing else, it is that we are going to have to take it all back again—every last scrap of it. Or rather we are going to have to co-operate fully with Aquarius as he prepares to wash it all away.

Until we have, there will be no more cake, no more apples—in fact, no more goodies at all. In short, it is tantrum time. But unfortunately no amount of childish tantrums is going to make the slightest difference. There is no parental magic to wish away reality. Instead, the time has finally come for us to grow up, to learn, and to take responsibility for what we have been and what we are. Only in that way is there the slightest hope that we shall ever become what we ultimately may be.

And perhaps it will indeed take **Edgar Cayce**'s polar shift, with all its associated devastation and destruction, finally to hoist the constellation of *Piscis Australis*—replete with all its eventual promise of a new, collective consciousness—above our nightly horizon.

2011–2015

• Date Summary •

Arrows indicate the beginning ↓ and end ↑ of a prophetic window

2011	↓	Beginning of window for humanity's descent to new spiritual low-point (*Great Pyramid*)
2012	↑	End of window for birth of Henri V of France (*Nostradamus*)
		Final death-knell sounds for France (*Nostradamus*)
2013	Jan/Feb	First spearhead of Muslim invaders penetrates south-western France (*Nostradamus*)
	↓	Muslim 'creeping' aerial bombardment of northern Europe begins—eventually destined to reach Britain and the Netherlands (*Nostradamus*)
		Possible death from illness of major Asiatic leader (*Nostradamus*)

2013	↕	Deep explorations into the earth's crust (*Arthur C. Clarke*)
	↕	New telesensory technologies developed (*Arthur C. Clarke*)
2014	↕	Mid-point of window for humanity's descent to new spiritual low-point (*Great Pyramid*)
	Aug	Murder of last Pope in captivity (*Nostradamus*)
2015		No specific events predicted

•COMMENTARY•

THE AQUARIAN AGE, THEN—OR AT LEAST ITS FULL BLOOMING—IS not yet to be. Before the dawn, as tradition has it, must come the darkest night. And in the present case that night is destined to be both physical and spiritual.

True, quite what the **Great Pyramid** means by a new spiritual low-point is not entirely clear. The development is indicated simply by a symbolic fall in the floor-level at the western end of its Great Subterranean Chamber (compare diagram p. 81). It could be a lowering of religious and moral standards. It could merely be the destruction of conventional religious institutions—which is not necessarily the same thing. It could be a decline in spirituality itself. It could even be a simple collapse of morale.

Not all of these would necessarily be totally disastrous. A lowering of religious and moral standards always tends to create a vacuum that eventually leads to a new revival and reinvigoration of both. A decline in spirituality tends to lead to a new hunger for things spiritual that might not otherwise have occurred. The destruction of conventional religious institutions—the churches, the priesthood, the ritual observances—can bring to the surface again that true spirituality that all three can so easily obscure.

This is clearly already the case in the modern West, following the virtual collapse of its earlier religious and spiritual certainties. To it we largely owe the popularity of the contemporary New Age movement, with its huge range of 'alternative' spiritual and psychospiritual practices.[14] Even more is it the case in contemporary Russia and its satellites, where the abrupt ending of up to seventy years of enforced state atheism has brought about a positive ferment of spiritual activity, both in the media and in society at large—ranging from the religiously orthodox at one end of the spectrum to the most extreme of occult manifestations at the other.

A further case in point will demonstrate the principle. The virtual—if unofficial—abolition of religious education in British schools has led to a quite unexpected result. Teachers report cases of pupils who, unlike most of their forebears, are actually prepared to read the scriptures of *their own accord*.

Oddly enough, then, the apparent collapse in general values that seems to be marked out for the second decade of the twenty-first century is actually a sign of hope. It is one of the very preconditions for a new revival, actually laying the groundwork for the new initiative of reform and reconstruction that **Nostradamus** assigns to the future French King Henri V, currently only in his infancy.

And the murder of the last of the Popes by his alien captors after some ten years of imprisonment—signalled by Nostradamus at *Century* I.52 for the summer of 2014—will, however tragic in itself, certainly serve as a resounding symbol of that collapse.

There are, then, better times to come. Indeed, help will eventually be forthcoming from a foreign leader to whom Nostradamus refers as the 'Provider' or 'Supplier'—conceivably the then President of the United States—while the name of young Henri himself, evidently baptised at some point between 2007 and 2011, has already been inscribed, as *Sixain* 38 reveals, upon the immortal scroll of human destiny:

'Midst mighty plague and flood and warfare grim
The great Provider, risking life and limb,
Shall show his mettle and reveal his face;
And in six-fifteen or six-nineteen they
Shall carve a mighty Prince's name for aye—
Fifth of that style—upon the Cross's base.

But much has to happen first. Things have to get much worse yet before they eventually get better. And it is Nostradamus's beloved homeland of France, alas, that has to bear the brunt of them.

The grim marauders from Spain

The Muslim invaders, it seems, take time to consolidate their hold on Spain. Advancing northwards and eastwards from their now well-established strongholds in the south—areas that had already been Muslim once before until shortly before **Nostradamus**'s birth—they eventually mass their forces in the Ebro valley between Pamplona and the river Duero, prior to attempting a crossing of the Pyrenees into south-western France. In this, as *Century* III.62 describes, they eventually succeed where the earlier, Tyrrhenian (i.e. Italian) wing of the invasion failed. One defending army is routed in the Pyrenees, while another retreats before the marauding hordes into the valley of the Aude and the French coastal strip stretching from Perpignan to Narbonne, leaving Carcassonne in particular exposed to all that the invaders can throw at it.

Here, however, as at Narbonne, the defenders put up a valiant fight, while guerillas continue to resist in the mountain passes (I.5). Even at sea there is renewed resistance, as the British at last come to the assistance of the French navy in the Mediterranean, using a startlingly familiar weapon (II.59):

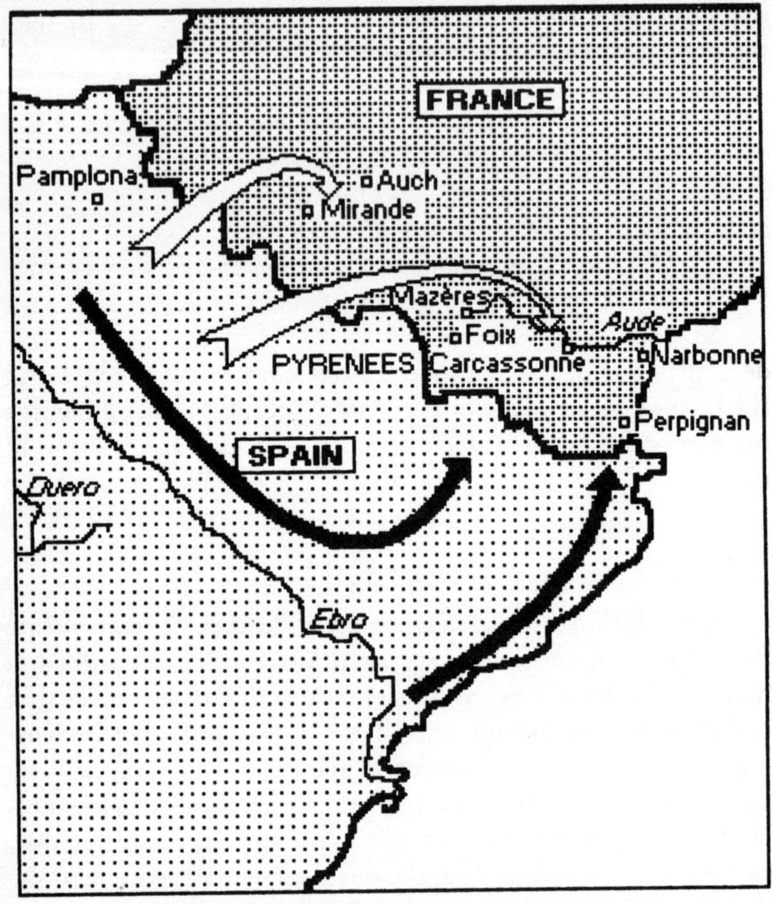

The invaders enter south-western France, 2013

Supported is the French fleet by the hand
Of Neptune and his warriors' Tridents tall.
To feed the horde Provence lays waste its land.
War at Narbonne, with missiles large and small.

Whether this means that the alarmed West now decides to resort to nuclear weapons in a desperate attempt finally to stop the invaders is not entirely clear. But the upshot is that the invaders now turn to similar weapons of their own. Again and again (as at *Sixain* 27, for example) Nostradamus describes fire falling from the sky, leaving the landscape positively aglow. The target-areas are left looking like a whole series of carbuncles—semi-mythical precious stones glowing fiery red by their own inner light. Carcassonne, Foix, Auch, Mazères—all suffer the same merciless treatment (*Century* V. 100).

It is shortly after this, consequently, that Nostradamus has the invaders entering Foix in the Pyrenean foothills (IX.73), dating the event astrologically either to 15–18 February 2009, 4–19 February 2011 or 20 January to 2 February 2013—and this despite the death of one of the invading commanders (IX.73, II.2). Of these three dates, the last seems the most likely in terms of what has gone before—and indeed, of what is now about to follow.

For the pattern is now set for the rest of the campaign. As the invaders move ever further northwards, the earth-shaking aerial bombardments will steadily precede them. In due course, consequently, this terrifying 'creeping barrage' of bombs and missiles that will already have devastated the 'Grand Old Lady' of France is set to reach Britain and the Low Countries as well.

Nostradamus hints at *Sixain* 54 that this may prove the last straw for the reluctant northern allies, at last provoking them into counter-attacking the invaders with all the force that they can muster. Previously thought to refer to the Second World War—and particularly to the London Blitz of 1940, on account of its superficial similarity of detail—this verse's obvious references to Nostradamus's 'liturgical count' in fact date the events described to the years 2007–12:

Six hundred fifteen, twenty, Lady dies.
Thereafter soon a great rain from the skies
Of fire and iron shall hurt those countries sore.
Britain is of their number, Flanders yet.
Long shall they by their neighbours be beset
Until to them constrained to take the war.

The situation so far

The circumstances at this point correspond remarkably closely to those foreseen by **Mario de Sabato**. This modern seer, too, predicts that a kind of 'left-wing fascism' will overrun the whole of the Mediterranean basin—though in his case he expects it partially to spare his beloved France, where it will, he says, find little response and so have less severe or lasting effects. This unexpected detail bodes well for his reliability—for it of course suggests that his vision owes nothing to the influence of **Nostradamus**. But then he also expects an enormous grass-roots *Chinese* influx—largely unarmed, and extending to much the same areas marked out by Nostradamus for the eastern wing of his own future invasion. This, says **de Sabato**, will help counter the totalitarian threat from the south and eventually result in an intermingling of the races, a cross-fertilisation of philosophies and a reorganisation of the whole of Europe on new foundations of equity and justice.

Jeane Dixon also expects a Chinese invasion. In her case she expects it to overrun Europe as far as the Franco-German border (she does not say from which direction, but the east is implied). Nevertheless, her vision is entirely compatible with **Mario de Sabato**'s. In which case one cannot help wondering whether both have not simply misidentified what is in fact the northern, or European wing of **Nostradamus**'s Asiatic invasion. For 'Chinese', in other words, read 'Mongol' (a term, as we have seen, that **Jeane Dixon** also uses of the invaders); and for 'countering the threat from the south' read 'squabbling with their southern colleagues'.

With this, as we shall see in due course, **Nostradamus** would certainly concur.

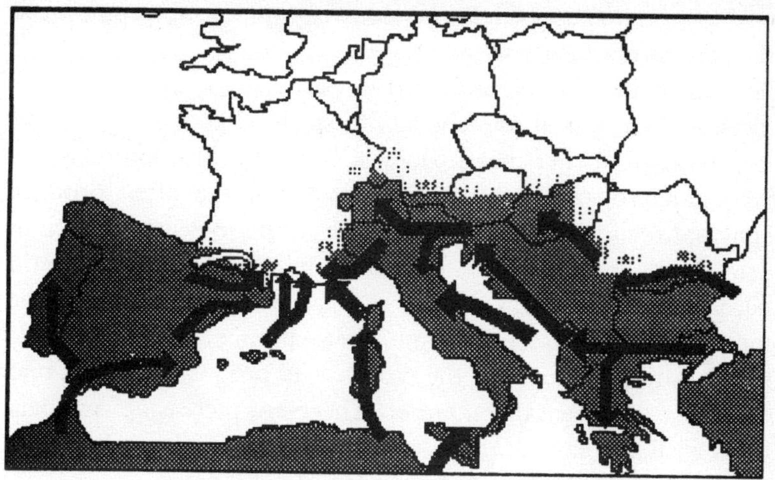

The Muslim invasion: progress up to 2015

The swings and roundabouts of fortune

So it is, then, that the beginning of the second decade of the century is set to mark not the dawning of a glorious new Aquarian era, but the onset of what may yet prove to be Europe's darkest hour. That darkness, it seems, is destined to be not merely physical, but spiritual too.

Nobody should be surprised at this. Comforting it may be to assume that the spiritual is somehow the reverse of the physical—even that it serves as a kind of compensation for it. But reality is not like that. It is simply not interested in instant compensations.

There is a related assumption, common among pseudo-educationists, for example, that all children are equally gifted, and that those who are not well endowed intellectually are compensated by increased physical gifts and skills. 'All men,' in other words, 'are created equal.' Any teacher will confirm that this is just not the case (if only it were so!). The cleverer children are generally also the tallest, the strongest, *and the best at sports and handicrafts as well.* Moreover, they quite often come from the richest families, too.

No, nature is not fair. And in particular it does not compensate for physical hardships with spiritual goodies.

True, the belief that it does is common. No doubt that is why dangerous or uncertain physical times so often produce spiritual revivals. People seek solace in religion, reassurance in firm creeds, motivation and security in promised heavens and paradises. The present day offers a clear case in point. In the face of the uncertainties of modern existence, religious fundamentalism is rife all over the world. And not just Christian and Muslim fundamentalism, either. There are increasing numbers of Jewish fundamentalists, Hindu fundamentalists, Buddhist fundamentalists, even Confucian fundamentalists.

To say nothing of New Age fundamentalists, all with their favourite, new-fangled creeds (however loosely defined).

But fundamentalism is not necessarily the same as spirituality. Indeed, it can actually prove inimical to it. The events described in this book bear ample witness to that.

And yet, in another sense, spirituality is not really the opposite of anything at all. In particular, it is not the opposite of physicality. For the universe is one and indivisible, and if we perceive it to have separate physical and spiritual aspects, then that is merely because our perception is selective.

Bringing heaven down to earth, in other words, is a largely pointless exercise. Heaven and earth were never separate in the first place, and are assuredly not separate now. It is the illusion that they are that lies at the root of much of our discontent, of our religious strivings, and consequently, too, of our religious wars and conflicts.

'The Kingdom of Heaven,' as Jesus is reported to have insisted, 'is already among you.'

So it is that, in the Europe of the future, as of any age, the physical and the spiritual will continue to go hand in hand. If things are going badly physically, then they will undoubtedly go badly spiritually as well, whatever the outward compensatory antics of those who would prefer this not to be the case.

The compensation—if compensation there is—lies purely in the fact that, in a polarised, dualistic world, it is the very crisis itself that will tend to provoke its opposite. The deeper the crisis, indeed, the more towering the eventual recovery.

2016–2020

• Date Summary •

Arrows indicate the beginning ↓ and end ↑ of a prophetic window

2016		First steps taken to control weather (*Arthur C. Clarke*)
2017	↑	End of window for humanity's descent to a new spiritual low-point (*Great Pyramid*)
	Jan	Muslim invaders succeed in crossing the Pyrenees in force, armed with chemical weapons (*Nostradamus*)
	↓	Aerial attacks prove the last straw for France (*Nostradamus*)
	Jul/Aug	South-western France attacked with more thermal weapons from the sky; the invaders penetrate French defensive lines on the river Garonne (*Nostradamus*)
	Dec	Narbonne falls to the Muslims (*Nostradamus*)
2018		No specific events predicted

2019	Jul/Aug	Alternative date for further thermal attacks on south-western France and fall of Garonne defence-line (*Nostradamus*) Possible death of a second oriental leader (*Nostradamus*)
2020	↓	A 'false oriental religious philosophy' invades the West, eventually prompting (by way of reaction) a return to primitive Christianity (*Jeane Dixon*)

•COMMENTARY•

IT HAS TO BE SAID THAT **ARTHUR C. CLARKE**'S TYPICALLY OPTIMISTIC forecasts seem more and more out of kilter with other predictions at this juncture. It may of course be that in parts of the world remote from the growing conflict—Japan and the United States, possibly (provided that **Edgar Cayce**'s geological disasters have not disrupted things there too severely)—technological developments of the types he describes will indeed be proceeding apace. And if so, then the ability to control the weather could bode well for restoring the world's food supplies once the great conflict is over. It could also have a direct bearing on humanity's future attempts to address the growing problem of rising world temperatures and sea-levels, as anticipated not only by Edgar Cayce, but by growing numbers of today's climatologists, too.[6]

In Europe especially, however, things are by this stage looking progressively darker as year gives way to year. **Nostradamus** spells out the details in his own graphic terms.[13]

With the whole of Iberia now firmly under the invaders' heel, all eyes are now on the south-west of France. Evidently the Muslim hordes are successfully held back for a time—which bespeaks a great deal of valour and determination on the part of the outnumbered French defenders, who are receiving pre-

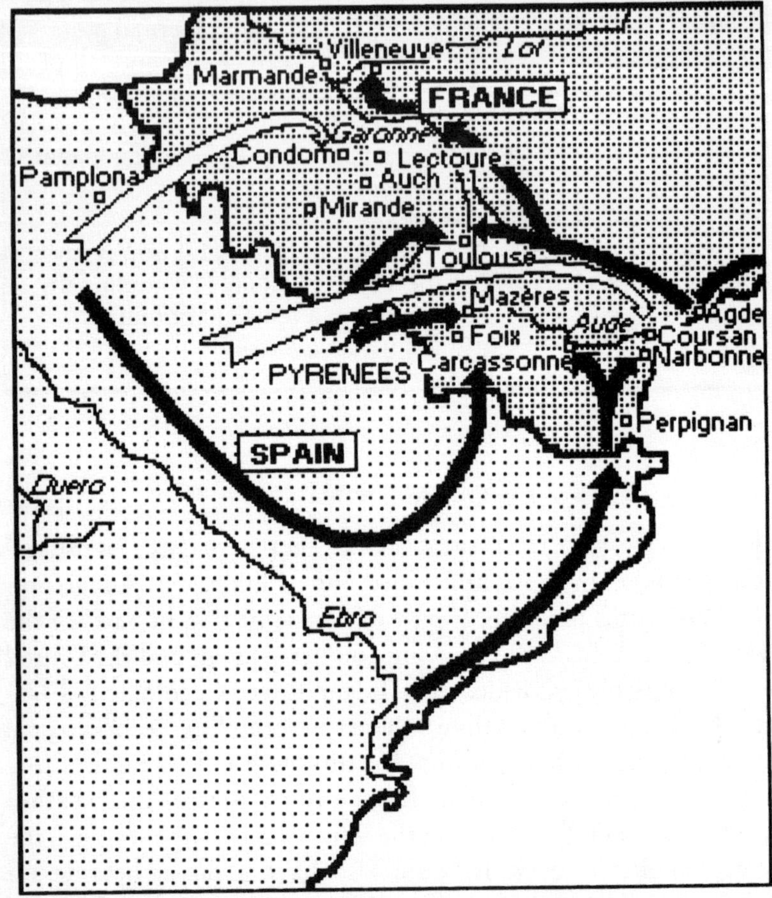

The south-west of France falls to the invaders

cious little support from the rest of Europe. True, there are some signs of German and Swiss assistance (*Century* IV.74), even though Switzerland itself is by now under occupation, while Germany is under attack from the south. But from Britain there is as yet little beyond sporadic naval support and a few encouraging noises.

Clearly the desire is still strong not to get involved in other people's wars. The spectre of returning body-bags is still too much for 'disinterested' governments such as the British to contemplate. Only when it starts to become obvious that, if one country falls, its neighbour will be next, are the defensive reflexes likely to start taking over—but by then it may already be too late.

Possibly it is this reluctance to intervene that convinces the invaders that now is the time finally to throw all their irons into the fire. With great determination, they thrust further powerful spearheads across the Pyrenees into France, deploying what has been called the 'poor man's nuclear weapon'—namely chemical artillery, based on technology long-since developed by countries such as Iraq. At II.48 Nostradamus dates this further development astrologically to late January 2017. As the invaders pour south-westwards out of the mountains and down the west bank of the river Aude, Narbonne is soon attacked and overwhelmed, so enabling the enemy to encircle and storm Perpignan (III.92, VI.56).

With further attacks in the offing (this time from the sea via Barcelona), there are now moves to stage popular risings in occupied towns such as Coursan and Narbonne, but Nostradamus warns strenuously against any such thing, even picturing the aerial attack on Perpignan that will assuredly follow any such action (VIII.22)—'*High-flying, grey, beflagged, your killer see.*'

For a while the French succeed in confining the Muslims to the west of the river Aude, but then the invaders succeed in outflanking the defensive perimeter by landing enormous numbers of troops from Barcelona at the little port of Agde, just behind the hard-pressed French defence-lines. According to *Century* VIII.21, the initial attack is mounted by no more than three assault-craft, but other troops then follow. Nostradamus places their eventual total number *at a million*, and envisages them taking three attempts to break out of their initial beachhead before they finally emerge to spread mayhem, destruction and pestilence all across the countryside.

The great break-out once achieved, the city of Toulouse is next on the list (VI.98). Here again, 'pestilence' is soon roaming the streets—this being one of a number of possible references to the invaders' use of germ-warfare. And soon the terrified citizens are watching their city being destroyed before their eyes, their churches sacked, their river and canal flowing red with blood. This action, indeed, proves absolutely catastrophic for the defenders: *Century* I.72 suggests that up to a million of them may be killed.

Thereafter, with the defence-forces devastated, the enemy advance starts to acquire a truly frightening momentum (XII.71), even though, as Nostradamus elsewhere reveals, the beleaguered French repeatedly attempt to use their various rivers (Aude and Garonne, then Lot and later Loire) as defence-lines:

Rivers and streams may slow the evil tide,
But anger's ancient flame will not be checked.
Through France as fast as rumour it shall ride:
House, manor, church and palace shall be wrecked.

The anti-Christian pogrom

One particular characteristic of the spreading invasion is that the Church is made a special target (*Centuries* IV.43, VI.9). The clergy are universally persecuted, their congregations murdered, their buildings razed to the ground. The invading troops are actually awarded medals for each grisly act of sacrilege—the more brutal the better. Indeed, the torments inflicted eventually reach such a pitch of severity that even the hard-bitten **Nostradamus** can only call them 'amazing'.

The seer makes exactly the same point in his dedicatory letter to King Henri II. The conflict, it seems, has a distinctly religious dimension that serves to render it, not more caring or more understanding, but—as was ever the case—ten times more inhuman and ferocious.

The future invaders, in other words, will seek to conceal all their murder and brutality under the cloak of zeal for Islam, despite the fact that true Islam enjoins neither action on its followers. The whole thing, in short, will be a prime example of religious bigotry and hypocrisy. But then religion, bigotry and hypocrisy have ever gone hand in hand, leaving far behind that true spirituality that was always the original object of the exercise.

No wonder, then, that the Roman Catholic **Jeane Dixon,** too, foresees the abandonment of Christianity in favour of what she terms a 'false oriental philosophy' that will increasingly come to contaminate it. This contamination, she insists, will largely be the work of the coming Antichrist (born, she insists, on 5 February 1962) who, basing his work in Jerusalem, will prove particularly seductive to the youth of the world until his baleful mission is eventually seen for what it is.

Mrs Dixon may well be right. But if so, her 'gentle Antichrist' is certainly not the same bloodthirsty monster and military leader who is envisaged by **Nostradamus**.

As for the 'false oriental philosophy', this too may be well predicted. Its 'falseness', though, may not lie so much in the fact that it is oriental and non-Christian (as **Mrs Dixon** herself seems to believe), as in the fact that its most militant proponents will not really believe or practise their creed at all. In the name of Allah the Compassionate, the Merciful, the most brutal atrocities will be committed, murder, rape and genocide be inflicted on all and sundry, weapons of the utmost horror be used with almost total abandon.

We have, of course, seen it all before. It was the Christian West, after all, that as long ago as the Crusades inflicted exactly the same catalogue of brutalities on the Muslims.

The nuclear dimension

And so it is perhaps no surprise that, from 2017 onwards (as *Sixain* 44 has already suggested), further aerial attacks are now mounted on those areas that are still managing desperately to hold out. This time, moreover, the onslaught looks as though it might be nuclear in character (*Century* I.46). Auch, Lectoure and Mirande are all subjected to a rain of fire from the sky that

Nostradamus calls 'stupendous and astonishing', and afterwards the earth quakes violently.

Later (at VI.34) Nostradamus actually identifies the source: he refers to it as '*Of flying fire th' ingenious machine*'. There can be no doubt at all, in other words, that it is a man-made device, and its earth-shaking nature seems to rule out mere laser weapons. Are we, then, talking about nuclear devices? It may well be. The only caveat is imposed by the fact that he describes the rain of fire as a continuous one lasting all of three nights. Could it be, then, that the weapon is one that has not so far been invented? Or are we, after all, merely talking about some kind of incendiary and high explosive attack?

The first of the major defence-lines crumbles

More 'fire from the sky' now descends on Condom, Auch and Mirande (VIII.2), while brilliant flashes accompanied by 'hail' are experienced at Marmande. It *sounds* like a mere thunderstorm, admittedly, but somehow one has the feeling that **Nostradamus** has much nastier things in mind. The date is 18 August 2019 (possible alternative astrological dates two years earlier and later do not seem to fit Nostradamus's sequence, though the former does look closer astrologically).

Faced with this onslaught, the French defensive line on the river Garonne totters, crumbles and eventually collapses, so allowing the invaders to swarm across it towards the north. With this the floodgates are finally opened, and all hell is let loose on the rest of France.

Villeneuve-sur-Lot is first in the firing-line (VI.97), and here once again thermal weapons are used. True, numerous commentators have been seduced by the seer's cryptic term *la grand cité neufue*—and, it has to be said, by their own credulity—into supposing that the 'new city' in question is New York. But Nostradamus specifies that it lies within the forty-fifth degree of latitude, which runs *some 300 miles north of the American city*. The contortions performed by the commentators to wave this fact away are often truly instructive—and ignore completely

Nostradamus's characteristic techniques for encoding place-names, one of which involves simply translating each element of the name into other words, often taken from different languages.

Cité neufue, in other words, is merely a typically Nostradamian reworking of *ville neuve*: and the only Villeneuve that fits his account at this point is Villeneuve-sur-Lot—which indeed lies within the forty-fifth degree of latitude. As any map of the place-names mentioned by the seer soon reveals,[13] his interests were confined almost exclusively to western and southern Europe, the Mediterranean Basin and the Middle East. America and the Far East scarcely figure in his account at all, still less the yet-to-be discovered Antipodes. A world-sage he may have been, but by and large his visions are limited to those areas most familiar to Frenchmen of his day, and to inhabitants of Provence in particular.

For to their future counterparts the coming Muslim war is destined to prove literally a matter of life and death.

The race northwards

Thus it is, then, that the marauders succeed in crossing the river Lot as well, subsequently racing northwards as fast as they can go across Aquitaine towards the next major French line of defence, on the mighty river Loire. This they duly reach in remarkably short order—and it is at this point that the British at last wake up to the danger fast approaching their own shores and start to intervene in earnest on the French side, using Nantes and Rennes as forward headquarters.

The siege of the river-girt city of Tours, augmented with further chemical or even biological weapons, seems to twang anxious British nerves particularly. At *Century* IV.46 the inhabitants are assured of British support, and warned to stay indoors all the while an evidently noxious 'drizzle' is falling from the skies.

It is all in vain, though. The hastily cobbled-together allied forces are simply no match either for the vast numbers or for the focused motivation of the bloodthirsty enemy. Forces from Switzerland, north-western France and Germany all assemble to face the military threat rapidly advancing northwards from Aquitaine (IV.74). But they prove no match for the advancing hordes, and are soon overrun.

With Tours, Blois, Reims and Angers thus faced with the prospect of a huge 'change' (**Nostradamus**'s familiar word for an out-and-out disaster), to say nothing of Orléans and Nantes, all of them are now first besieged, then occupied by the enemy. And soon the mighty pincers of war are closing around Paris itself, while Brittany, too, is under aerial attack. Rennes in particular (no doubt because it is the defenders' regional headquarters) undergoes an earth-shaking missile bombardment (I.20).

Indeed, it is at this point that one of the most charismatic of the defending leaders is killed by one such attack near Fougères. The event is evidently seen as having huge symbolic importance, for Nostradamus devotes two quatrains to it (IX.19, 1.26), as well as two of his *Sixains*. *Century* I.26, indeed, links it with the start of a bacteriological assault on Britain and northern France:

In daylight broad a bolt shall fell the lord—
So does this humble messenger predict.
As long foretold, too, night sees war abhorred
London, Reims, Tuscany with plague afflict.

As *Sixain* 31 goes on to suggest, the effect of the death on public morale is enormous:

He who o'er all life's hazards shall have soared,
Nor ever feared or fire or flood or sword,
A native of the country round Toulouse,
Shall by the Crocodile be stricken down
Through warlike act of wondrous great renown.
The folk shall be agog to hear the news.

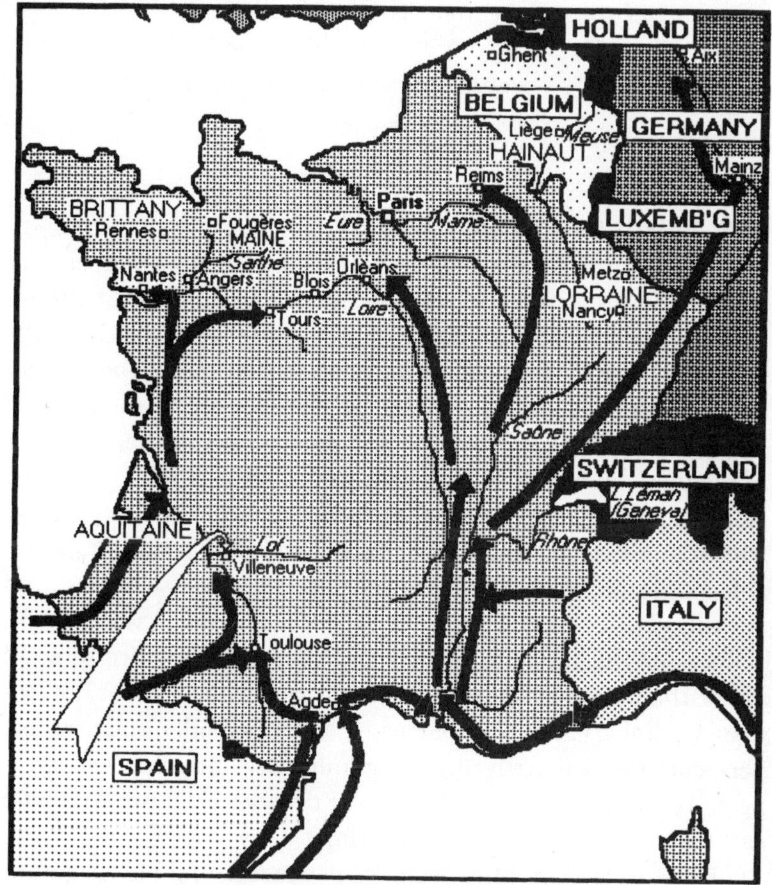

The invaders pour northwards

But then there are also signs at *Sixain* 45 that the shock of it may be such as eventually to galvanise the reluctant defenders—and especially the British (constantly characterised by the sceptical Nostradamus as the 'Leech')—into taking decisive action of their own, whatever its final outcome may be:

A blow of steel shall all the world amaze,
Dealt by the Crocodile in curious ways
To a great kinsman of the Leech, and peer;

And soon thereafter, as in ambuscade,
Shall yet another 'gainst the Wolf be laid,
Though of such deeds the outcome be unclear.

New moves on the eastern front

By this time, meanwhile, there is an even worse turn of events: the hitherto relatively dormant Italian wing of the invasion stirs into action once again, pressing northwards up the valleys of the Rhône and Rhine. Soon (much to the further alarm of the British) its reinvigorated forces are at the gates of Nancy and Metz, led by a commander who is either 'another Alexander' or merely Greek by origin (X.7). Cock-a-hoop, he gloats publicly over his coming victory, while the British are tempted to turn to drink for solace. Even the Germans are unable to protect their own territory to the west of the Rhine, and with the fall of Mainz seem set to lose Cologne as well (V.43).

As for the Italians, French and Iberians, they are now all under the most brutal form of enemy occupation, with the Roman Catholic Church in particular systematically undermined, persecuted and destroyed throughout the continent. The prospects are truly gloomy as the decade draws to a close. And who can say what its successor will bring?

Who, indeed, but the prophets in general, and Nostradamus in particular?

Pause for breath

Clearly, then, the moment of darkest night is fast approaching. All hell has almost literally been let loose in Europe. Total defeat is staring the beleaguered West in the face. To Westerners, who habitually think in straight lines, alarm and panic are the almost inevitable reactions. If things are getting steadily worse, after all, surely they can only continue to get steadily worse?

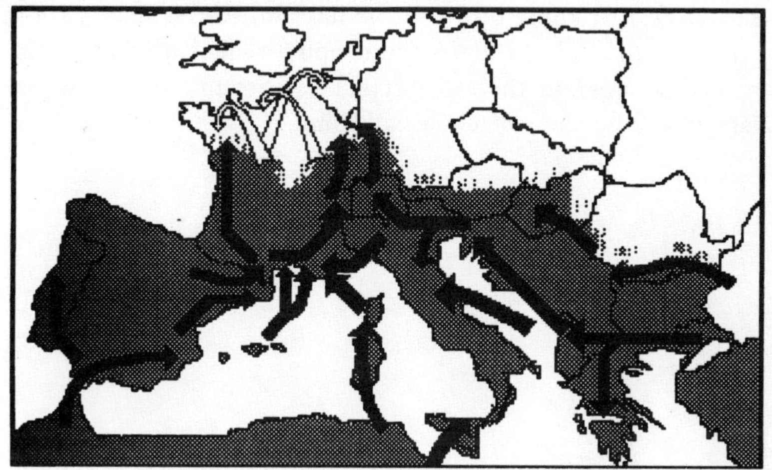

The Muslim invasion: progress up to 2020

Orientals in general, and the Chinese in particular, are often much wiser in this regard. Preferring to think in terms of cycles, they tend to be worried less by bad times than by good. If things are going well for you now, they argue, then watch out—for they can only get worse. If, on the other hand, present circumstances are about as bad as they can get, cheer up—for the likelihood is that they will soon start to get better.

Thanks to the same kind of logic, too, they are less concerned with 'improving the world', since they realise that no such improvement can last, even if it does not actually make matters worse in the first place. They do not come up with theories of existence, either, that see humanity as proceeding in a straight line from the biblical Creation to the End of the World. And advocates of science's corresponding Big Bang theory and the expanding universe, with its similarly straight-line view of existence, notably do not come from China.

Perhaps, then, we should learn from the orientals' wisdom, be it Chinese or Muslim. Perhaps, indeed, it is precisely this deeper wisdom which (unknown even to themselves) will be the invading hordes' last and best gift to us, much as **Mario de Sabato** suggests—for all the inevitable horror and mayhem that they are set to inflict on us in the interim. And if that wisdom is part of the 'false oriental philosophy' that is destined to inform and supplant the more typical Christian view, then perhaps it will not be entirely a bad thing.

2021–2025

• Date Summary •

Arrows indicate the beginning ↓ and end ↑ of a prophetic window

2021	Feb	Muslim invaders reach Luxembourg and a flooded Lorraine (*Nostradamus*)
	↑	End of window (initially opened in 1993) for start of initial, 'Progressive' period of new Golden Age; new respect for scholars and learning at the expense of mere politicians; immense scientific advances for the benefit of civilisation generally (*Mario de Sabato*)
2022	↓	Beginning of window for partial re-establishment of civilised societies (*Great Pyramid*)
	Feb	Muslim overlord officially installed at Reims and Aix-la-Chapelle (Aachen); Asiatic empire reaches its furthest extent on Belgian border and English Channel coast (*Nostradamus*)

Year		Event
2022	Mar	Severe disease epidemic hits France: up to two thirds of population and livestock eventually wiped out (*Nostradamus*)
2023		No specific events predicted
2024		No specific events predicted
2025	↕	Mid-point of window for partial re-establishment of civilised societies (*Great Pyramid*)
	↓	Following would-be peace negotiations, 'Red' China invades Russia, eventually overrunning Scandinavia and reaching the Franco-German border (*Jeane Dixon*)
	↑	Reinvasion and liberation of France by combined Western forces from Germany and Britain (*Nostradamus*)
	↕	New interstellar probes launched, while on earth robots are coming into their own (*Arthur C. Clarke*)
	↕	Genetic science starts to be applied to the task of improving inherited characteristics (*Arthur C. Clarke*)

•COMMENTARY•

AFTER THE WHIRLWIND EVENTS OF THE PREVIOUS FIVE YEARS, IT might be thought that things would start to slow down a little during the third decade of the century. But not a bit of it. If anything, the pace is set to be even more frenetic than before. On the other hand, not all the events that do occur are likely to be quite so irredeemably gloomy as before. Indeed, there seems to be considerable light at the end of Europe's long, dark tunnel.

Both **Mario de Sabato** and the **Great Pyramid**, after all, see signs of a newly dawning age of gold, or at least of reconstruction. **Arthur C. Clarke**, too, suggests a whole range of resplendent new technological developments. With robots taking over much of our menial labour, and possibly many of our less menial tasks, too (as indeed has already started to happen), humanity will be progressively freed to look beyond earth towards the wider cosmos, while also turning its attention to improving its own bloodline and consequently its general health and well-being too.

At the same time, though, his hinted use of genetics to 'improve' the human race sounds rather ominous. Disturbingly reminiscent of Hitler's notorious eugenics programme, it offers boundless opportunities, after all, for selective interference in the natural reproductive process for the exclusive benefit of one's own tribe or group. If nothing else, then, any such development will demand a prior increase in human benevolence and philanthropy. Humanity, in other words, is going to need to be freed from the cruder and less helpful aspects of its animal inheritance—and this, unfortunately, is unlikely to be something that can be brought about by genetic manipulation, at least for a good while yet.

But then, as so often, perhaps science will surprise us.

Nostradamus, too, meanwhile, seems a good deal more optimistic than before. While admittedly predicting further advances by the Muslim invaders of France as far as the borders of Belgium and the English Channel, he at least goes on to anticipate the beginning of moves to expel them again. And even **Jeane Dixon**'s predicted Chinese invasion might—if both she and **Mario de Sabato** are to be believed—eventually have a part to play in the liberation process.

Mario de Sabato's picture of the impending new world order is particularly encouraging. As time goes on, he suggests, humanity will learn to access knowledge directly in some as-yet unexplained way that was unknown to earlier generations. Possibly he is referring here to world-wide computer-networking, which had of course barely been dreamt of at the time he made the prediction. Computer-technology might also explain his further forecast that manual labour will be largely abolished in favour of mere responsibility for overseeing automated processes. The agreement with **Arthur C. Clarke**'s robotics forecast is striking.

In time, too, the human lifespan will be extended—and not merely by extending old age, but by actually prolonging the full vigour of youth. Whether or not as a result of Clarke's genetic manipulation, ageing will (according to **de Sabato**) become a fairly brief process starting at about age fifty-five, with ninety-five a by no means unusual age. Winter will be largely abolished—despite the inevitable problems that this change will also bring—thanks largely to the work of Russian scientists (one wonders, too, what part continued global warming will play in the phenomenon). And terrestrial agriculture will increasingly be supplemented by marine farming.

In the meantime, though, there is much unfinished business to be got through. And it is this that, as usual, Nostradamus can be relied upon to detail for us.

The triumph of Islam

We left the invading Muslim hordes heading pell-mell northwards across the river Loire in the west, and down the rivers Meuse and Rhine in the east, their mighty pincers preparing to close on Paris itself. By 2–18 February 2021, in fact, the eastern forces, like the rising waters themselves, are flooding into Lorraine and Luxembourg, as **Nostradamus** almost playfully reveals (*Century* X.50):

Saturn plus three within Aquarius
The Meuse and Luxembourg by day shall hail,
Flooding Lorraine, cities and strongholds various,
Mountains and plains. Bucketfuls of betrayal!

Indeed, one wonders once again whether **Edgar Cayce**'s major inundations are not part of the general picture at this time.

A little to the west, Reims is apparently under chemical attack (III.18). Following a 'long rain', something that looks suspiciously like milk falls from the sky upon the beleaguered city. As a result, while a bloody battle is raging all across the surrounding countryside, the invaders are not too inclined to set foot in the city itself. Indeed, they do not need to.

And so it is not long before the French capital, too, is under attack by the enemy overlords, secure in their remote Roman headquarters. Foreign troops, says **Nostradamus** at *Century* V.30, are soon billeted in every town and farm, while within the city itself enormous casualties are suffered by both sides as the invaders attempt to cross the various bridges over the Seine. But resistance is to no avail: indeed, as verse II.63 explains, all it does is to guarantee annihilation. Here as elsewhere, the invading hordes are far too numerous for the defenders. These are simply overwhelmed, and the great city duly falls.

This traumatic event is, of course, of major symbolic significance for the invaders. But they are not about to stop there. With the fall of Paris and—as it subsequently turns out—its virtual destruction, all the territory between Paris and the English Channel now lies open before the enemy. Accordingly, they go on not only to besiege and take Rouen, but to advance to the Belgian frontier itself (IV.19). Hainaut and Flanders both seem to be threatened with imminent invasion, as is the region of Liège, where only the natural barrier of the Ardennes seems to stand in the enemy's way.

With virtually the whole of France overrun, the invaders' triumph is complete. As though to rub the point home, the Asiatic overlord now arranges to be welcomed and officially installed in power during the course of what appear to be traditional coronation ceremonies at Reims and Aix-la-Chapelle—the latter no doubt intended to recall the glories of the reign of the former Emperor Charlemagne. In *Century* IV.86 Nostradamus dates this development astrologically to the first week of February 2022.

Such resplendence is merely the opposite side of the coin of human ruin and abject misery, however. Throughout France especially the Church is wiped out, its priesthood virtually exterminated (VIII.98):

> *The blood of churchmen shall be freely shed:*
> *Long time shall pass ere it shall cease to flow.*
> *As though 'twere water see it flowing red!*
> *Woe, ruin, grief the priests shall undergo.*

Following the sudden, traumatic death of the great war-leader referred to in the previous section, the last of the ruling élite have hurriedly fled the 'Grand Old Lady' of France for Britain and America, in many cases (as *Sixain* 35 reveals) leaving their families behind them:

> *How sad that death shall make the Lady be—*
> *Mother and tutor—as the leaders flee,*
> *Ladies and lords, each child of theirs a waif!*
> *The mighty Crocodile and deadly Snake*
> *Shall forts and castles, towns and strongholds take.*
> *May God from such marauders keep them safe!*

And meanwhile the country itself is not merely devastated, but racked with deprivation as well.

But the new occupiers determinedly do nothing about it. Soon (VII.34, IX.55) there is virtually no bread, salt, beer, wine or medicine, and even unpolluted water is hard to come by. Not only is much of the country consequently afflicted by hunger and cold, but within a year (as if all this were not enough) a ghastly disease epidemic strikes the weakened survivors, killing off further millions of humans and animals alike. In fact, the astrology of IX.55 suggests that this may occur as early as 7–11 March 2022.

Nostradamus does not identify the pestilence—he certainly does not call it the Plague—but its effects (combined with those of the invasion itself) are truly horrific. Up to two thirds of the

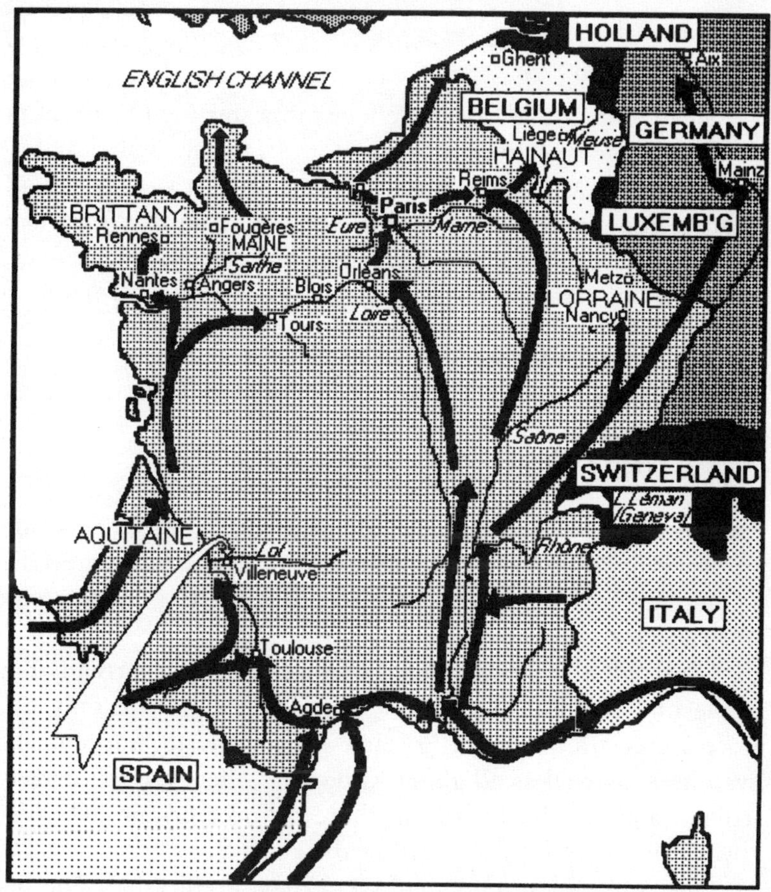

The invaders reach the English Channel

population of France (as he details in his dedicatory letter to King Henri II) are wiped out, leaving whole towns and cities deserted, houses empty and farmlands untended. Grass (he predicts in a telling phrase) will grow knee-high and more in the city streets. No wonder that the seer foresees a time when mourning and grieving are virtually universal, and light-heartedness of any kind decried as if it were some kind of blasphemy.

England at bay

Meanwhile the invaders are inevitably starting to turn hungry eyes in the direction of England itself, which is already under bacteriological attack from the air (I.26). At *Century* VI.43 **Nostradamus** warns the British not to imagine that they can beat the invaders once they have landed. Far better, he implies, to keep them firmly at bay:

Long time unpeopled shall the country lie
That's watered by the rivers Marne and Seine.
Tempted the armies England are to try:
Folly to think to beat them back again!

Fortunately, however, quarrels and dithering on the enemy side intervene in Britain's favour, and a last-minute hitch prevents the already massing invasion-force from getting under way (V.71).

Quite what that hitch may be is not clear. But virtually the whole of Latin Europe is now at its last gasp, with only the more inaccessible parts of Brittany apparently still unoccupied. Even here, as well as all along its borders, there are murderous artillery and air attacks, just as there are over Britain, which is now of necessity fully engaged in the conflict.

One result of Britain's engagement is predictable. The invaders proceed to try, like various would-be conquerors before them, to starve the islands out. Nostradamus, as ever, refers to the then Britain (towards which he still seems to harbour distinctly ambivalent feelings) as the 'Leech', but nevertheless seems to approve of the fact that it will be saved from starvation in the nick of time by a foreign 'Prince' whom he elsewhere describes as the 'Supplier' or 'Provider'—and who seems to be none other than the USA or its President. He refers to this development both at IV.15 and at *Sixain* 7:

The Leech the Wolf shall join in war
When wheat by sea is needed sore,

But the great Prince its pleas shall heed:
He'll send a mission to supply
Wheat of his own lest it should die,
That it may satisfy its need.

At this point, though—as ever, just when the night seems to be at its darkest—there are sudden signs of hope. At long last the Western worm seems to be about to turn. Britain in particular is already rapidly rearming (*Century* III.71). And as a result, the prospects for the future are starting to look a good deal more promising (*Sixain* 50):

Before or after straight shall England lie,
Through Wolf laid low, prostrate and fit to die.
Then shall the fire against the water rise.
Relit, it shall increase its strength and power
And human hearts shall superhuman tower.
Of food not much; of weapons vast supplies.

On the European mainland, similarly, massive forces are beginning to assemble to mount a mighty counter-invasion from the north-east (*Century* V.13):

The lord from Rome in furious anger black
Shall send his Arab horde Belgium to rape:
But just as furious they shall chase them back
From Hungary to stern Gibraltar's cape.

Indeed, it is virtually certain, as we shall see, that the counter-invasion is already well under way before the end of the current period, as Nostradamus sees France liberated by the spring of 2026.

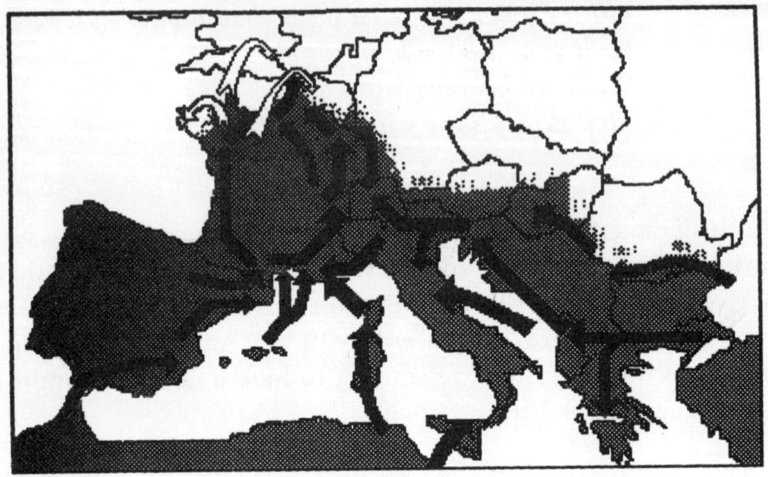

The Muslim invasion: progress up to 2025

A sense of 'déjà vu'?

We have, of course, been here before. Those familiar with British history will recall a whole series of similar foreign invasion-threats going back to the time of Napoleon and beyond. The coasts of southern England are littered to this day with lines of so-called 'Martello towers', built to help stave off the French as recently as the last century.

More than any other events, the circumstances described by **Nostradamus** nowadays seem evocative of those of the Second World War, in which a beleaguered and largely isolated Britain led by Winston Churchill hurled defiance for some two years at Hitler's so-far victorious forces—largely because there was precious little else to hurl. So similar are the circumstances, indeed, that numerous past commentators have become convinced that Nostradamus's predictions refer specifically to the time of the celebrated Battle of Britain. A number of details, however—and not least the seer's newly decoded dating information—effectively scotch that possibility. *Sixain* 54, in particular (see p. 113)

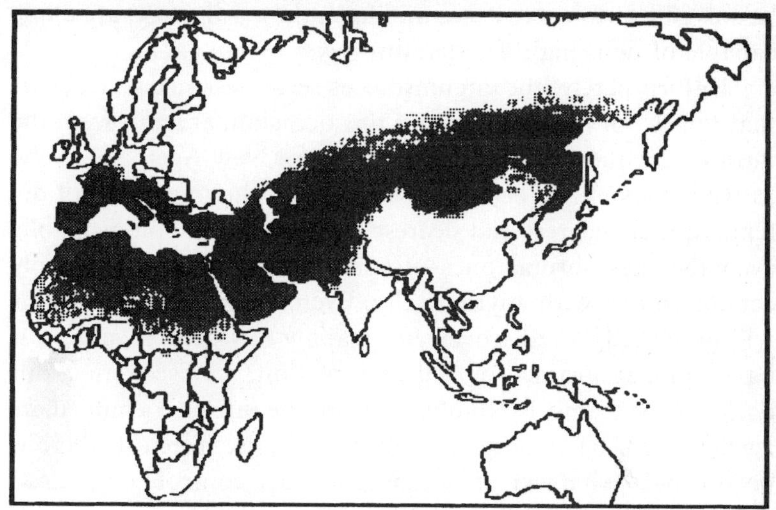

The Muslim empire: probable extreme world-wide extent

makes it clear that the events described are indubitably for our future, not our past.

Nevertheless, history has a way of repeating itself, especially all the while we fail to learn from it. Nostradamus, clearly, was convinced of this. Indeed, the notion goes right back to biblical times, when no less a figure than **King Solomon** is alleged to have penned the celebrated line in *Ecclesiastes* that runs: '*Whatever is has been before, and whatever shall be has been before, and God summons back again everything that happens.*'

If so, then we are in a position not only to be warned by what happened before, but to take heart from it. Certainly that is what is likely to happen. People will hark back to that last occasion and deduce (rightly, if **Nostradamus** is to be believed) that the time has come to rearm and, in the immortal words given by Shakespeare to Henry V at Agincourt, to 'stiffen the sinews, summon up the blood'. It will be a time for defiance, for belligerence, even for out-and-out aggression.

Inveterate pacifists, naturally, will not like this idea at all. New Agers will tend to agree with them that violence cannot be solved by violence. Peace and love, they will insist, are alone capable of defusing the situation.

Unfortunately, the circumstances seem designed to teach us that this is not the case. Not on *this* occasion, at least. Even the most determined pacifists and the mildest New Agers are likely, as we have seen, to be faced with the absolute necessity of defending their nearest and dearest with every weapon available, even the most brutal ones—for suicidal shock-troops simply cannot be met with anything else. Even the most civilised of us will be forced to rediscover and reapply our deepest and most basic animal instinct of self-preservation. Rediscovering our dark side, it seems, is Number One on the universe's immediate agenda for us. For until we have fully rediscovered it, there is no prospect whatever of bringing it under control of the new, developing, global consciousness.

There is simply no running away from it. The problem has to be faced. And perhaps it is because of this that the universe has seemingly arranged for there to be virtually nowhere to run to, either. It will, for example, be of no use at all for people from the south of England to flee to Scotland, Wales or Ireland, for biological warfare knows no frontiers. America, both North and South, will (if **Edgar Cayce** is to be believed) still barely have recovered from the enormous geophysical cataclysms of twenty years before; all over the globe, as present-day climatologists affirm,[6] sea-levels will be rising rapidly, so threatening many of the world's major cities and coastal lowlands; and (if **Mario de Sabato** is to be followed) severe financial difficulties will be affecting even the few safer areas that **Cayce** indicates.

Scandinavia may seem a better prospect, but will still be seriously affected by all the European mayhem, to say nothing of all the biological and possibly nuclear fallout. Much of Africa will no doubt be afflicted, as ever, by wars and political upheavals—to say nothing of disease epidemics. The Far Eastern countries of the Pacific rim, from New Zealand to Japan and beyond, are likely still to be prey to the severe geological disturbances to which the area is prone, even leaving out the likelihood of an eastward extension of the Islamic invasion. And if

Australia seems marginally safer, the possibility still remains of wide-spread droughts and/or floods.

As the biblical prophet **Isaiah** graphically puts it, once again in chapter 24, '*The hunting-scare, the pit and the trap await you, all you inhabitants of the earth. Run from the sound of the scare and you will fall into the pit: climb out of the pit and you will be caught in the trap.*'

No, this time the problems are going to have to be faced. And possibly that is why **Mario de Sabato** can see this as the beginning of what he called the 'Progressive' period of the dawning Golden Age. Reality, it seems, is starting to bite. The lessons are starting gradually to be learned, largely because there is no alternative. Realisation is starting to dawn. Little by little, the psychological ground is being prepared for a general acceptance that things can no longer be allowed to go on like this. Something must finally be done.

Having frightened ourselves virtually to death, we in the West shall at last have the necessary motivation to take ourselves by the scruff of the neck, recognise ourselves for what we are, and take the necessary steps to transform ourselves into what, if we are to survive at all, we ultimately have to become.

2026–2030

• Date Summary •

Arrows indicate the beginning ↓ and end ↑ of a prophetic window

2026		Assassination of Asiatic overlord (*Nostradamus*)
	Apr	France liberated (*Nostradamus*)
2027		Counter-invasion of Italy (*Nostradamus*)
2028	↑	End of window for re-establishment of civilised societies (*Great Pyramid*)
	↓	Northern allies back in control of both France and Italy (*Nostradamus*)
	Nov	French leader assumes supreme power in Europe (*Nostradamus*)
2029	↓	Beginning of window for humanity's recovery from its spiritual low-point (*Great Pyramid*)

2030	↓	Sudden, unexpected emergence of a former much-admired peacemaker as a powerful warlord to combat 'the Red Chinese menace' in Russia and Scandinavia (*Jeane Dixon*)
	↑	End of window for invasion by 'false oriental philosophy' (*Jeane Dixon*)
	↕	World temperatures and sea-levels rising rapidly (*John Gribbin et al.*)[8]
	↕	Mineral riches of space start to be exploited (*Arthur C. Clarke*)

•COMMENTARY•

QUITE WHAT PROMPTS THE BRITISH AND THEIR ALLIES TO STAGE their massive counter-invasion against Europe's Muslim occupiers at this particular juncture is not clear. But there are signs in **Nostradamus** that the Muslim confederacy will by this stage be falling apart in feuds and quarrels. At the same time the northern powers—possibly including the USA—will be drawing closer together and forming firm alliances. **Mario de Sabato** even suggests that *Chinese* support will be forthcoming. **Jeane Dixon**, on the other hand, seems to suggest that, on the contrary, the ever-advancing Chinese will continue to be the main enemy at this time, and that the outside help will come from an unidentified leader—albeit a flawed one—who may well be an American, formerly well known for his peace-making activities.

Either way, Britain is so clearly at risk from any further Muslim advance that attack may, as usual, be thought the best form of defence. And with the invaders temporarily at odds with each other this seems to be the perfect moment to strike. But then there is every sign that by the beginning of this particular period the great counter-attack will in fact already be well

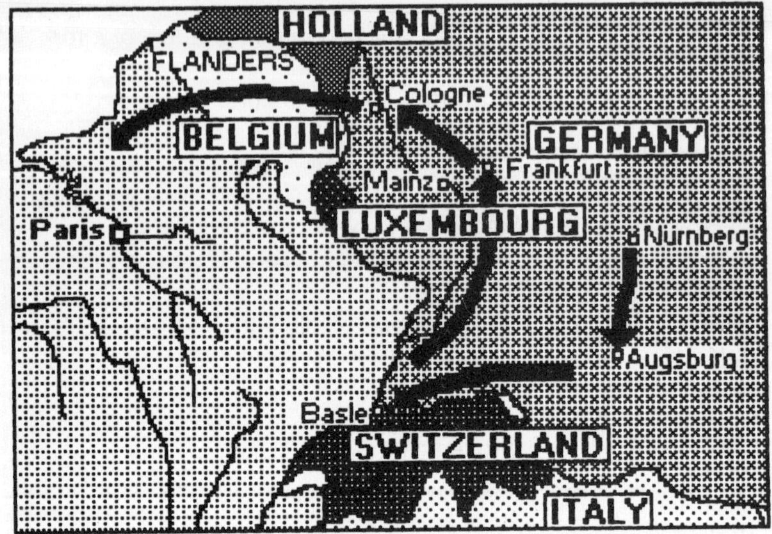

The counter-invasion begins

under way. **Nostradamus** does not actually date it—it has to take place at some time between 2022 and 2026—but he describes it in graphic terms that readers will find fully reflected in my earlier verse-translation.[13]

The great counter-attack

The initial attack seems to be mounted from Germany (*Century* III.53). Advancing southwards down the east bank of the Rhine, newly reinforced armies from the region of Nuremberg, Augsburg and Basle succeed in retaking first Frankfurt, then Cologne. Next they swing westwards and, taking the traditional invasion-route through Flanders, succeed in re-entering France. Having thus drawn the bulk of the Muslim defenders towards the north-east, the Western allies, from their headquarters in the west of England, now plan a surprise sea-borne invasion, not on the Normandy beaches, but on France's far west coast (V.34). A massive fleet is assembled on the British west coast, and it duly descends on the Gironde estuary with a whole arsenal of deadly weapons.

The enemy appear to be taken completely by surprise. The occupiers based in Bordeaux and La Rochelle put up a desperate fight, but an alliance of forces from Britain, Brittany and the Low Countries soon succeeds in overcoming them. On the northern front, possibly with the aid of further landings on the Channel coast, the defenders under the control of Rouen are pushed back to the river Loire, and specifically to the town of Roanne, which lies only a few miles to the north-west of Lyon itself (III.9).

In France's far eastern provinces, too, the invaders are on the run. Expelled from Lorraine, they are successfully besieged at Langres, but evidently leave behind them a bitter legacy of dissension and hatred. *Century* II.50 reveals that wars and quarrels based in ancient history now break out in the hinterland, such as to make even the miseries of the former occupation seem rosy by comparison.

Soon the counter-attack has reached Switzerland where, following what appears to be a nuclear and chemical exchange, the Europeans eventually succeed in driving out the occupiers. **Nostradamus** describes a 'mighty stench' arising from Lausanne as the aliens are finally driven out beneath fiery, almost apocalyptic skies (VIII.10).

Deaths and entrances at the top

It is at this point, some time during 2026, that the main Asiatic overlord at last falls victim to a palace coup after some twenty-seven years of world-wide mayhem. *Century* VIII.77 (which could almost as easily refer to Hitler or Stalin) reads:

The Antichrist is very soon laid low.
Seven years and twenty shall his battle stand.
Dissenters dead, captives to exile go.
Blood, corpses, reddened water pock the land.

The Muslim supremo, it seems, falls victim to an attempted assassination by an Arab soldier with an ambitious mother (VIII.73), and even though he does not die at once, he eventually succumbs to the effects of the poison that he has been given. As he lingers, dying, he blames the massive defeats now being suffered by his outnumbered forces on everything from internal sedition to heavenly retribution (II.47). But it is all to no avail. Death duly supervenes, and Europe's alien occupiers are plunged into despair.

As is almost inevitably the way of things, however, while one side of Fortune's wheel descends, the other mounts in equal degree. On the allied side, a mighty French leader now emerges whom **Nostradamus** refers to as 'Hercules'—or rather as 'Ogmion' (the ancient Gallic equivalent). One of his first successes takes place at Bourges, where he manages to defeat the great enemy general whom (as we have seen) the seer persists in describing as though he were another Alexander the Great (IX.93)—and this despite the latter's apparent use of a strong force of tanks.

In the west, meanwhile, things have not been standing still either. The initial British attacks on the Gironde estuary quickly succeed in establishing a beach-head and, outflanking the selfsame enemy general, the liberators succeed in joining up with 'Hercules' in the south-west of France before pressing on eastwards to liberate the rest of the country (IX.38, IX.85). Nostradamus describes actions near his old stalking-ground of Agen, as well as around a seriously subverted Narbonne. Thanks to further battles at Marmande and La Réole, Guyenne and the Languedoc are liberated and the river Rhône crossed, so opening up the whole of Provence to the advancing allies. Following further clashes near Vincent Van Gogh's former asylum of St-Paul-de-Mausole, to the south of St-Rémy, the liberators eventually go on to re-enter a largely ruined Marseille and restore it to its former life and vigour.

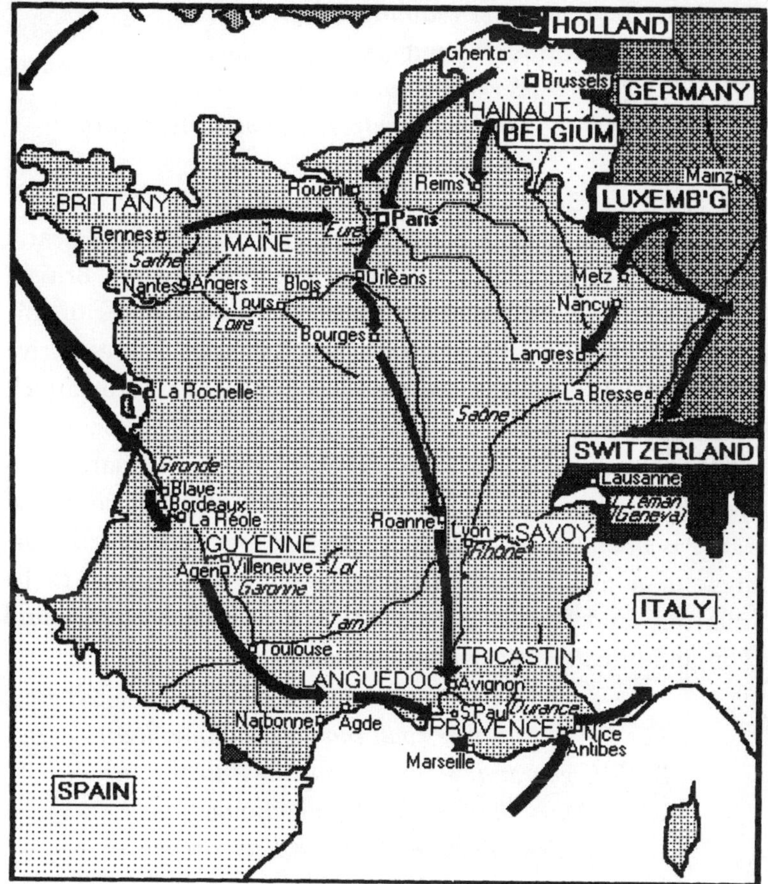

The liberation of France

The allied leapfrog strategy

By now, however, with the natural barrier of the Alps at their backs, enemy resistance appears to be stiffening. The Muslims even manage to recapture Provence from the allies. As **Nostradamus** puts it at *Sixain* 43:

> *This little spot, the Provinces once risen*
> *The military shall once more imprison*

With mighty castles looming everywhere.
In short, they shall a mighty siege endure
Till a great leader sets them free for sure
Who shall the land have entered through Beaucaire.

And so the northern allies concoct a brilliant plan to outflank their opponents with a daring naval assault via the Balearic Islands (*Centuries* V.51, VII.10, X.87). Romanians, British, Poles and Czechs all combine forces for the purposes of this escapade, whose first target is the isle of Majorca. This objective once achieved, they go on to mount a furious sea-borne attack on the French Riviera, occupying both Nice and Antibes.

The strategy is a complete success. And so it is that, by 16 April 2026 (the astrology is quite specific), this last corner of France is liberated from 'Babylon's yoke'—as well as from the threat of a new, British occupation—by what appear to be American land forces, after a murderous final battle around Lyon and in eastern Provence (*Sixain* 46):

The Great Supplier shall put to headlong flight
Both Leech and Wolf (or hear they me aright)
When Mars shall in the Ram conjoinèd be
With Saturn, and dread Saturn with the moon.
Then, with the sun aloft at blazing noon,
The nadir of your fortunes you shall see.

France's long run of ill-fortunes, consequently, at last bottoms out. At *Century* III.99 Nostradamus describes a massive engagement just east of his own home-town of Salon-de-Provence, somewhere between the villages of Vernègues and Alleins (which lie just south of the river Durance) and the Lubéron area (which lies just north of the river). And as a result the aliens are finally expelled from France.

At which point, with Paris in ruins, 'Hercules', his eyes already set on further conquests in Italy, sets up his new national capital not in Lyon, as its inhabitants had evidently hoped, but in the ancient city of Avignon (III.93, VIII.38). And so, despite the murderous battles that are continuing to rage in the mountains to the east, 'Blois's king' (as Nostradamus calls him, in the light of his apparent links with the former French royal family) establishes himself in considerable comfort, retaining for his own personal use four residences by the Rhône, to say nothing of the further home that he will subsequently establish at Nola, near Naples. This tendency to personal extravagance and even corruption is one that, as we shall see, will in due course get him into a good deal of trouble.

Not that the process of liberation is without other setbacks, either. In the south-west of France particularly, the invaders have long since intermarried with the local population and their languages have become intermingled (as Nostradamus reveals in his letter to Henri II, and **Mario de Sabato** confirms). The occupation, after all, has lasted over twenty years. And perhaps it is because of this that their local councils—notably those of Toulouse and Bordeaux—no doubt encouraged by the Muslims who are still in control just over the Spanish border, resolutely refuse to lie down before the liberators' new administration, which locally amounts to a British occupation regime. Despite desperate international efforts at conciliation, a violent civil war ensues, with much spilling of blood.

The reinvasion of Italy

However, the quarrel is eventually settled—more by brute force than by negotiation—and 'Hercules' prepares to invade Italy both by land and sea (VII.31, IV.23). Largely British liberation armies from the Languedoc and Guyenne, as well as French ones from Savoy, combine to force a passage through the Alps on the orders of their headquarters at La Bresse, while a British maritime task-force attacks Genoa with murderous fire-weapons. Soon, with the region around Milan liberated, the reinvasion has acquired more than enough momentum to take

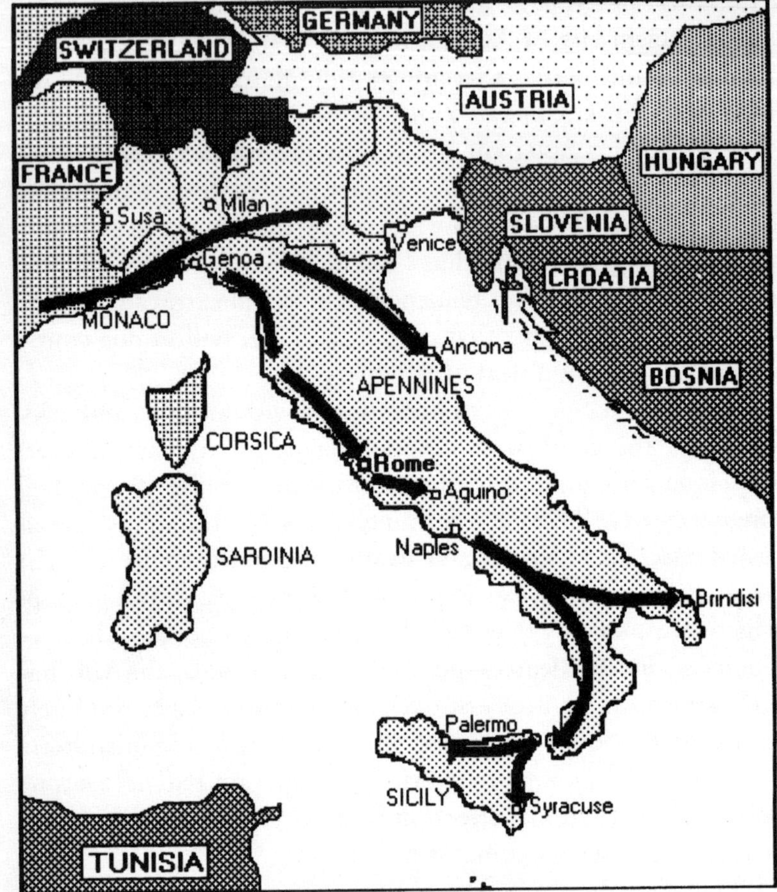

The liberation of Italy

it to the very toe of Italy and beyond. Realising this, the occupiers at last begin a hasty withdrawal by sea back to their heartlands to the east (IV.37). And even this, as *Century* V.80 reveals, will not be the end of things:

Hercules shall the might of Islam face:
Routed shall be the pagan dispensation.
The Muslims' mighty league away he'll chase,
Yet foe and free prolong their confrontation.

Prophetic warnings—and their futility

Nevertheless, **Nostradamus** warns the allied forces not to get too far ahead of themselves: they are likely, he suggests, to find that the retreating enemy still has sharp teeth. His warning is likely to go largely unheeded, however. And consequently, once the liberators from all over the French south-west have crossed the Apennines, they will run into unexpectedly stiff enemy resistance, as a result of which thousands of them are likely to die near Rome and the east-coast port of Ancona.

And so it will eventually fall to the bearded successor of 'Hercules'—who, as we shall see, is to be none other than the long-awaited King Henri V of France—to erect a memorial to the thousands who will needlessly die as a result (III.43).

This warning function of prophecy is one that Nostradamus attempts to apply again and again. Indeed, it is probably the mainspring of his whole opus, just as it is of those of **Jeane Dixon** and **Mario de Sabato**. 'They need not occur,' says the American seeress of the various man-made disasters she predicts. If people know in advance what is likely to be the outcome of their actions (all three prophets seem to have thought), then there is at least a chance that they will take appropriate preventive action. They might mend their ways, cleanse their thoughts, curb their appetites, rein in their greed, moderate their xenophobia, recognise their own intolerance. And failing that, at least they might pressurise their politicians to act in time to circumvent the coming crises, and urge their generals to prepare suitable defences.

Yet, in the very same moment that **Nostradamus** entertains such thoughts, he seems to concede that they are far too optimistic. People will change anything and everything, but the one thing that they will resolutely refuse to change is themselves. Only when they have no choice in the matter will they do anything so drastic as actually reforming themselves—and by then it will be far too late.

True, the lessons will be learnt in the end—but not as the result of mere warnings. As every wise parent knows, fingers actually have to be burnt before the truth finally sinks in that fire really is hot.

Europe liberated

Nevertheless, within some six months of the great slaughter, the Western allies are back in control of the whole of Italy. **Nostradamus** appears to date this development to the late summer or autumn of 2028. 'Hercules' himself takes over control of most of Western Europe from Rome in the south to Denmark in the north (II.16, IX.33), while from Naples on the Italian mainland to Palermo and Syracuse in Sicily, it is forces from Britain and the Low Countries who will be more prominent. By November, however, 'Hercules' is recognised as supreme ruler of the whole of Western Europe, and he now proceeds to exercise his new-found power to forceful and even terrifying effect, while at the same time showing much political skill (VI.42):

To Hercules the kingdom shall revert
Of the Great Muslim, mighty though he be:
O'er Italy his power he'll exert,
Ruling with most expedient subtlety.

There follow attempts to re-establish basic civilised institutions in France and Italy—in this case rather after the old Roman imperial model—and to reinstate the papacy in Rome. This latter initiative, however, runs into implacable political and military opposition, and the attempt has to be abandoned following the poisoning of the first would-be Pope of the new succession. On the positive side, however, some extraordinary archaeological discoveries are being made among the ruins of Rome as postwar reconstruction finally gets under way.

Meanwhile a further political and military crisis is about to develop. An attempt by a powerful rival to dethrone 'Hercules' on the grounds of vast corruption (described at VII.33) is set to result in a civil war that will shortly spread most of the way

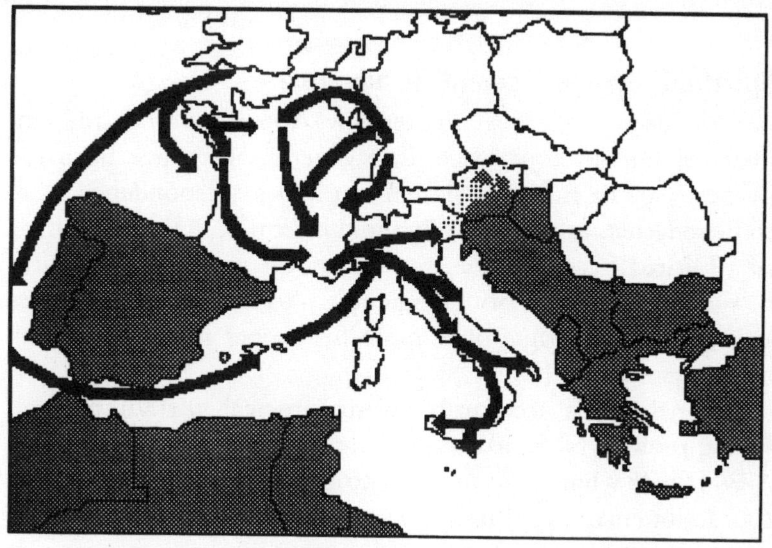

The European counter-invasion: progress up to 2030

across liberated Europe (see next chapter). Whether either figure has any connection with **Jeane Dixon**'s predicted peacemaker-turned-powerful-warlord who emerges at this juncture is not easy to determine—especially as she associates him with a military campaign against the *Chinese* forces that are by now supposed to be advancing from the East. Even in the benevolent, largely unarmed form that **Mario de Sabato** attributes to them, after all, these new invaders seem to be completely unpredicted by **Nostradamus.**

Civil war, then, or Chinese invasion? Revolutionary warlord or former peacemaker turned defence-chief? At present, at least, such questions simply cannot be answered at all reliably. All that can be said is that a period of severe civil and military turbulence is likely to follow the final expulsion of the Muslim invaders from France and Italy.

But then perhaps this is not too surprising. When, after all—for all the hopes and ideals of those who take part in them—did the aftermath of wars ever turn out to be other than hell on earth?

Spiritual recovery, scientific advance

Yet, as ever, there is brighter news, too, if in rather different areas of human experience. The general emergence from the deepest part of Europe's slough of physical despondency is set to be reflected, as the **Great Pyramid** indicates, in the beginnings of a spiritual recovery, too. Freed from the immediate pressures of sheer survival and of finding enough to eat, Europe's peoples will start to find time once more for deeper matters affecting their very souls.

Not that this necessarily means a revival of traditional religion, though. **Nostradamus** indicates at V.79 and II.8 (see pp. 173–4) that what will now start to occur is a deep questioning (no doubt encouraged by the recent encounter with the Orient) of the very nature of human beliefs and ideals—a questioning that will eventually lead to a genuine new beginning, both in attitudes and in practice. No longer will it be a matter of set church rituals, of easy verbal formulas, of rich vestments and precious ornaments and magnificent church organs. In the spirit of Matthew 6:5–8, hypocrisy will be recognised for what it is and flung unceremoniously out through the surviving stained-glass windows. Instead, the new religion of Europe, though still basically Christian, will find its sources in the humble and unpretentious—yet at the same time adventurous and open-ended—communal practices of the early Church.

As in spirituality, so in science. With efforts continuing to breed out of humanity those inherent flaws—physical or mental—that most stand in the way of the race's further evolution here on earth, all eyes will be turned on the opportunities increasingly offered by deep space. As the earth's sea-levels continue to rise and ever more of the coastal lowlands and major cities sink beneath the waves,[6] it is natural that people should look elsewhere for their salvation. And so the search will be on once again for valuable minerals on asteroids and other planets, as well as for signs of life elsewhere in the galaxy. If, after all, we can detect it, *ergo* it must have survived, and if it has survived, then quite possibly it has much to teach us, so that we can be sure of surviving too.

Both tendencies—spiritual and scientific—are understandable. When you are living in the midst of hell, the most obvious place to look to is heaven.

2031–2035

• Date Summary •

Arrows indicate the beginning ↓ and end ↑ of a prophetic window

2031		A third Asiatic leader drowned or burnt to death (*Nostradamus*)
2032		Young new French leader—the future Henri V—marries; floods in France (*Nostradamus*)
	June↕	European civil war begins (*Nostradamus*)
	↕	Mid-point of window for humanity's recovery from its spiritual low-point (*Great Pyramid*)
2033	Apr↓	Expected return of biblical Messiah (*Bible*)[8]
2034	Jan/Feb	Allied forces sweep across southern Spain (*Nostradamus*)
		Muslim invaders finally expelled from Spain (*Nostradamus*)

2034	↓	Beginning of ten-year period of postwar recovery (*Mario de Sabato*)
	Oct	Messiah's imminent return signalled (*Great Pyramid*)
2035	↑	End of window for humanity's recovery from its spiritual low-point (*Great Pyramid*)
	↓	Effects of Age of Aquarius possibly start to bite (*Aeonic astrology*)
	↕	Bioengineering starts to become wide-spread (*Arthur C. Clarke*)
	↓	Development of new cosmo-magnetic propulsion technique permitting remarkably easy space travel (*Jeane Dixon*)
	↕	First contacts made with extraterrestrials (*Arthur C. Clarke*)

•COMMENTARY•

IT IS FROM AROUND THIS JUNCTURE PARTICULARLY THAT VARIOUS of our sources start speaking of some kind of Messianic or pseudo-Messianic visitation. To take the **Bible** for a start, Jesus of Nazareth made it quite clear that he would reappear as King-Messiah 'three days' after his crucifixion. In all probability he meant it quite literally.[8] But in view of his manifest failure to do anything of the kind—for even Christians still await his re-appearance as world ruler—the New Testament's first letter of **Peter** suggests that each 'day' should really be read as a thousand years. The Messiah, in other words, will reappear at the beginning of the third 'day' of a thousand years after Jesus' death—which would place the Messianic return at any point from the spring of 2033 onwards. (Compare the **Great Pyramid**'s revelations on p. 175.)[11] Indeed, since the Jewish expectation was always that the Messiah would return at Passover, we can possibly be even more precise about it. The so-called Second Coming—the advent of the heavenly Messiah of the dawning Aquarian Age—is due on or after *14 April 2033*. Which is almost exactly a year-and-a-half before the **Great Pyramid**, too, expects (on 31 October, to be precise) some kind of Messianic 'sign' to appear, possibly in the sky.

Quite what form either phenomenon will take (even if we accept the possibility in the first place) is, of course, extremely difficult to anticipate. **Arthur C. Clarke,** for example, suggests that the first human contact with extraterrestrials might also take place at some point during this period—and no doubt the representatives of any truly advanced civilisation from outer space would seem to us little less than gods. Indeed, this seems to be precisely the form in which **Mario de Sabato** expects the eventual 'Messiah' to appear—though he places this particular event much later in time (2163 at the earliest). **Nostradamus** seems to have similar ideas for the far future, though they are much more difficult to decode.

However, Nostradamus, like **Mario de Sabato** (see his prophecy for 1999), does also offer us tantalising glimpses of a related event much closer to us in time. For (curious though it may seem) he predicts the appearance of a remarkable new leader in Europe who will indeed have a kind of Messianic aura about him—*and this at almost exactly the date seemingly anticipated by both the* ***Bible*** *and the* ***Great Pyramid*** *for the proclamation of the Messianic return.* The future King Henri V (or 'Chyren', as **Nostradamus** calls him in suitably anagrammatic terms) will have been born and raised in humble circumstances well out of the limelight (*Century* V.41), and will succeed the powerful but corrupt leader known as 'Hercules' by 2034 at the latest, after the latter has been defeated and mortally wounded as a result of the Europe-wide civil war (IV.95, V.23, VI.58, VI.95, II.34, V.64, VI.7, V.45, II.38, VIII.5). The astrology of

Century V.23 seems to pin down the beginning of this conflict to the first week of June 2032.

Young though Henri is, he will turn out to be an extraordinarily charismatic and powerful leader (IV.14). At *Sixain* 38 (page 111 above) Nostradamus dates his baptism to some time between 2007 and 2011, while at *Sixain* 4 he confirms this by placing his birth astrologically at some point between 2010 and 2012:

Of Orb and Lily's born a monarch great,
Sooner or later bound for high estate
(Saturn in Libra in high exaltation,
Fair Venus' house's influence wearing thin),
Of female looks, but male beneath the skin,
For blessed Bourbon line's continuation.

Directly descended from the ancient royal line of France, but also with an admixture of German and other blood (V.74, V.39), Henri it is who will finally manage to push the Muslim invaders out of Europe and back to the Middle East, as well as restoring the Church to its former eminence. He will also, if *Sixain* 40 is to be believed, put an overbearing Britain (the 'Leech'), whose troops are currently lording it somewhat in Europe, firmly back in its place:

With what in life his father never knew
By fire or sword he shall himself endue
And shall the disputatious Leech rebuff.
His full inheritance he shall possess
(For God Immortal shall his efforts bless),
His rightful Province gaining soon enough.

And as a result (*Century* V.41), a veritable new Golden Age will dawn in France, and possibly in the rest of Europe as well.

True, there seems to be powerful outside participation in the liberation-process, too. At *Sixain* 56, as elsewhere, Nostradamus seems to expect this to come from the United States (a possibility also floated by **Mario de Sabato**), applying to it the cryptic label 'Provider' or 'Supplier' (*pourvoyeur*, which I have elsewhere translated as 'Steward'), while referring to Henri (who is, after all, the leader of an international force) as the 'Griffon'—a composite mythical beast that is part-lion (Britain?) and part-eagle (Germany or Italy?). The African Muslims, by contrast, he refers to as the 'Elephant', and their Asiatic allies (as ever) as the 'Wolf':

When the Provider joins the Griffon's side
The Elephant shall everywhere abide.
Its ruin near, and dread Mars roaring still.
Griffon shall wonders work near Holy Land,
Great banners fluttering over sea and sand,
Once brothers twain on Church have worked their will.

The whole idea of a charismatic new royal advent in France may seem distinctly optimistic, of course, but the insistence with which **Nostradamus** keeps returning to the theme leaves little doubt as to his convictions on the matter—convictions, it has to be said, that mesh in closely with the popular expectation among modern-day French royalists that just such a figure as Henri, possibly descended from the ancient Merovingian kings—or at least from the later Bourbons—will one day appear to restore the pre-1848 monarchy and become the latter-day saviour of France.

The liberation of Spain

Henri now takes further steps to subdue the rebellious south-west of France, and then, after what seems like a period of combined negotiation and threat, starts to pursue the anti-Muslim campaign down into Spain, finally reaching the south

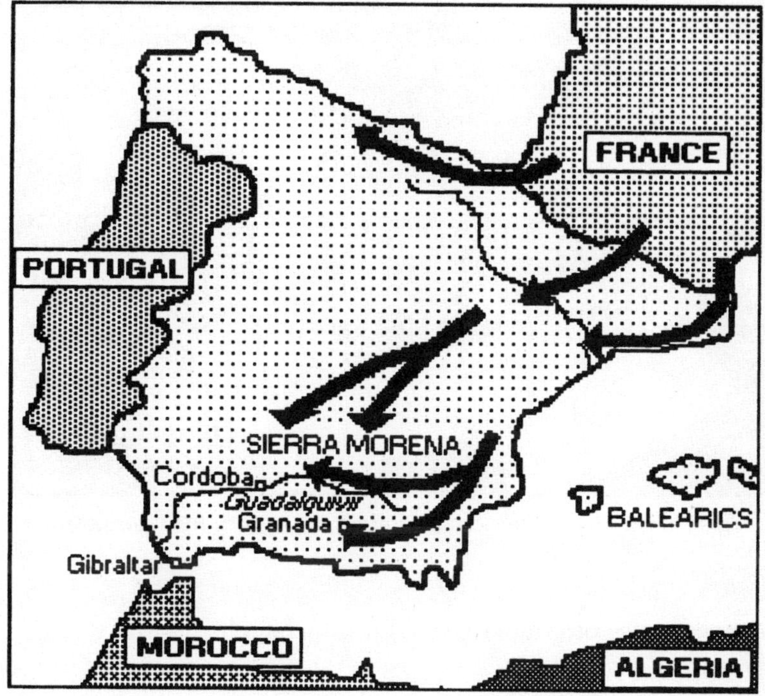

Henri's forces push into Spain

of the country in early 2034 (*Centuries* X.95, VIII.48). There are decisive battles both at sea and on land. Finally, a furious triple assault is mounted on the Sierra Morena, and the Muslims ('those who Friday keep', as **Nostradamus** calls them) are successfully driven out of Spain and back into North Africa, just as they were once before, some half-a-millennium previously, shortly before the French seer's birth.

But then Henri seems to have been campaigning in Spain since at least 2032, for it was in that year (when Saturn was leaving what, to it, was an 'unfavourable' sector of the zodiac) that he seems to have married there, taking his bride from the Spanish branch of the ancient Bourbon line of kings (here described, in traditional, optimistic vein, as descendants of the

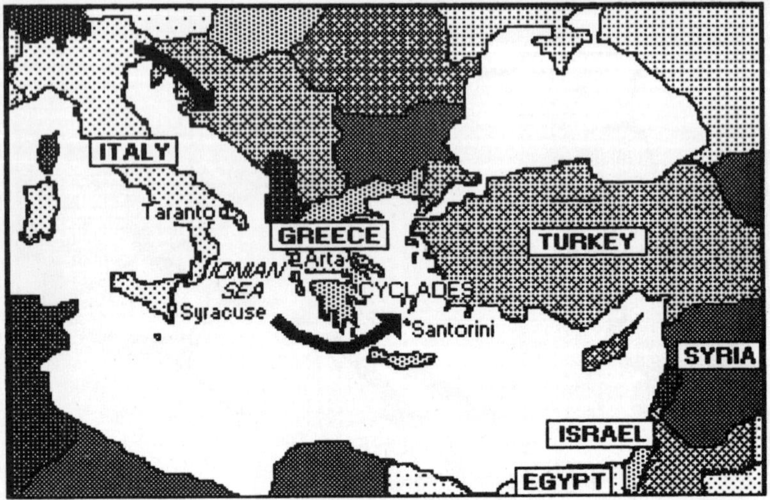

The allies extend their campaign into the eastern Mediterranean

ancient house of Priam of Troy) from which he himself was also descended (V.87):

The year that Saturn shall his serfdom quit
Shall Frankish lands by floods be stricken hard.
With Trojan blood a marriage he shall knit,
While Spaniards shall provide a bodyguard.

The allies return to the East

Yet, as *Century* IV.5 reveals, this is by no means to be the end of the fighting:

Christians and peace and Holy Writ fulfilled,
Both France and Spain under one king united,
The host at hand, fierce combat, many killed,
No heart so brave as not to be affrighted.

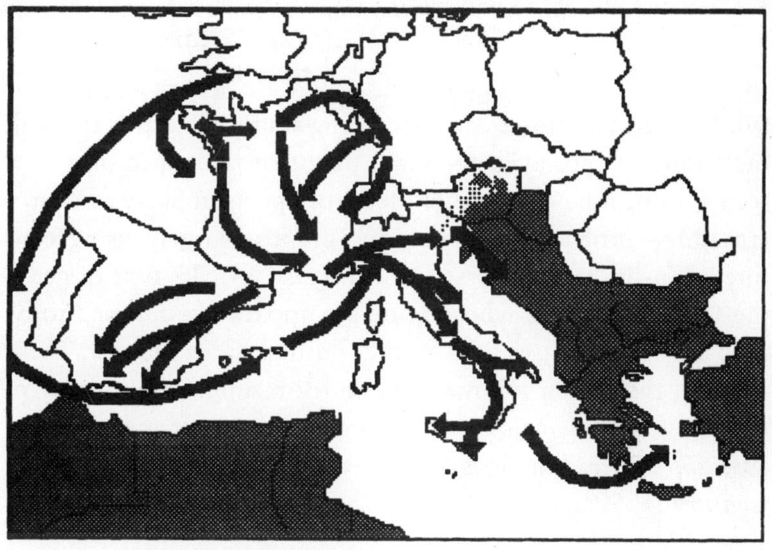

The allied counter-invasion: progress up to 2035

For Henri now turns his eyes towards the Middle East and, despite a good deal of pacifist opposition from his homeland (itself newly stricken by severe floods that are once more somewhat reminiscent of **Edgar Cayce**'s predictions, to say nothing of those of present-day climatologists),[6] prepares to launch a mighty expedition to chase the Muslims all the way back to their Asian heartlands. The campaign is to be an international one, and so (as previously) **Nostradamus** invokes his familiar cast of Griffon and Provider pitting their strength against the Muslim Elephant and Wolf (X.86). *Sixain* 39 in particular seems to heap praise on the Americans for their part in the action:

On monster worse than any other one
The Great Provider glowers like the sun
Ascending towards its zenith at midday.
In routing Elephant and Wolf at last

He'll triumph more than any monarch past:
Let ne'er this Prince's glory fade away!

While allied land forces are advancing south-eastwards through the former Yugoslavia, the main thrust of the expedition is, it seems, to be a naval one mounted from ports in Sicily or southern Italy—probably Syracuse or Taranto—largely using captured Muslim supply-vessels (*Century* III.64). Its first target is the Greek Cyclades, whose ports are apparently destined to be used as forward bases for a further push towards the east. These secured, there then follows a pause for resupply and reinforcement before the major assault begins. Nostradamus gives no date for either, but does suggest the vaguest of timescales at *Century* IV.50:

Autumn shall see the West's full power deployed,
Dominion wielding over land and sky:
Yet none shall see the Asian power destroyed
Till seven in turn have raised the sceptre high.

This last line corresponds to the earlier prediction in *Présage* 40 referring to the very beginning of the Muslim invasion—a verse that reads:[13]

Seven kings in turn death's deadly hand shall smite,
Hail, tempest, plague and furious desecrators:
The Eastern King shall put the West to flight
And subjugate his former subjugators.

This might suggest, then, that from the start of the Asiatic campaign in 1998 or 1999, France will know seven successive presidencies. With the presidential term currently set at seven years, and the first presidential elections after 1998 due in 2002, this would suggest an end to the conflict in around 2044. On the other hand, resignations and/or deaths could well bring this forward somewhat, so that a date in the late 2030s actually seems the best bet. Since **Jeane Dixon** dates the end of what she calls the 'Chinese war' to 2037, this consequently seems a reasonable date to accept.

In which case the concluding stages of the war—and Henri's eventual title to some kind of Messianic claim—are for us to examine in the next chapter.

The skyward gaze

And yet the first steps, however faltering, have been taken towards the creation of a new world. A new leader and a new regime—Messianic or not, but certainly of a much more encouraging stamp than previous ones—are promising a new start in Europe. Religion is being refounded on new bases. In science, major steps are being made to 'force' human evolution by genetic means. A new idealism is in the air. Astrologically—or at least astronomically—the new Aquarian Age is knocking at the door.

And so perhaps it is no surprise that, spiritually as well as scientifically, eyes all over the world are increasingly turning heavenward.

The search has long been on, after all, for signs of life elsewhere in the cosmos. Somehow, as we have already observed, it seems to offer us some hope that we shall survive—some guarantee that, despite all the evidence to the contrary, we *can* actually survive. Now, according to **Jeane Dixon**, new propulsion techniques are starting to make it possible for us to penetrate deep space with remarkable ease. The probes, both manned and unmanned, are pressing further and further out into the unknown, always searching, always sending out their questing impulses.

And then, at long last, very weak to start with, the first response. Somewhere in the depths of space, some other civilisation—possibly even more advanced than the most civilised on earth—has picked up our faint signals, has recognised them for what they are and has replied. Across the light-years, the first, tentative, electronic handshake reaches out. The great vision of **Arthur C. Clarke** and a thousand other science-fictionists is fulfilled.

The knot—and with it the future—is sealed.

2036–2040

• Date Summary •

Arrows indicate the beginning ↓ and end ↑ of a prophetic window

2036		No specific events predicted
2037	↑	Invading 'red' Chinese forces finally halt their advance on the Franco-German border (*Jeane Dixon*)
	↕	Beginning of 57-year period of peace and prosperity (*Nostradamus*)
2038		No specific events predicted
2039	Oct	Initial, semi-Messianic figure appears (*Great Pyramid*)
2040	↕	Communication established between humans and intelligent animals (*Arthur C. Clarke*)
	↕	First steps in transmutation of elements into one another (*Arthur C. Clarke*)

•COMMENTARY•

AND SO IT IS THAT THE LONG PERIOD OF PROFOUND CRISIS FOR Europe—and, indeed, for the world as a whole—at last promises to draw to a close. **Jeane Dixon** speaks of a Red Chinese invasion that has moved through northern Russia and is now fast approaching the Franco-German border, but she has little else to say about it. (She is, after all, a part-time seer who specialises in isolated snapshots, rather than connected scenarios.)

The more full-time **Nostradamus**, for his part, seems to be well ahead of her, if on a different track. According to him, the Muslim invaders have already been rolled back from the whole of western Europe, and now Henri and his allied forces, fiercely determined at long last to put a stop to the whole sorry episode, are poised to begin the final assault to free the eastern Mediterranean as well.

Its preparations complete, the allied fleet sets sail from Taranto and/or Syracuse in huge numbers. The Muslim high command (including the celebrated 'second Alexander' whom we have repeatedly encountered before) knows perfectly well that its last hour is at hand (*Century* VIII.81):

Desolate shall their empire new become,
Changed by the power that far to northward lies.
From Sicily a mighty change shall come
To wreck the Macedonian's enterprise.

Fittingly, perhaps, the first landings are made on the Greek and Albanian west coasts, where Henri's forces go on to discover that Greece, the former homeland of the original colonisers of Provence, is in urgent need of humanitarian relief (I.74). The emergency appears to be general: Nostradamus mentions both Arta on the west coast and Thrace in the north-east (IX.75).

Next, the combined fleets, sailing from ports as far apart as

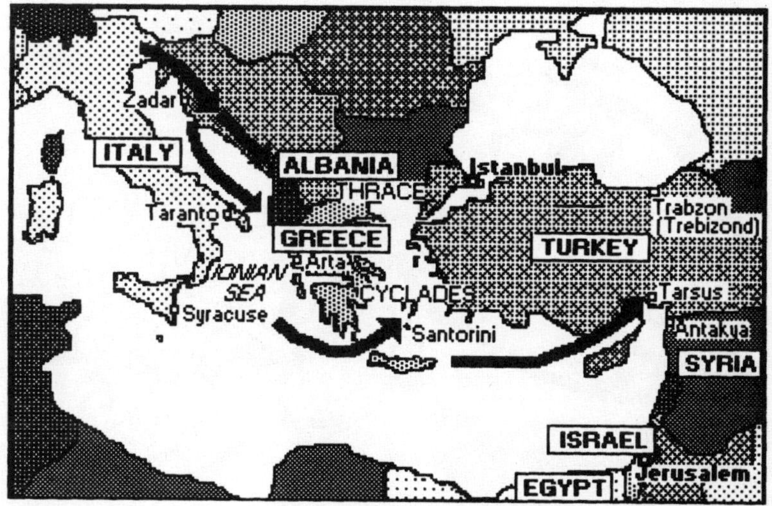

The final assault on the Middle East

Syracuse in Sicily and Zadar on the Dalmatian coast of the now liberated former Yugoslavia (VIII.83), mass near the sunken volcano of Santorini, in the already reconquered Cyclades, for a mass attack on the Turkish mainland:

The biggest fleet that ever Zadar knew
Near Istanbul its deadly business plies.
Great losses to the foe; to friends but few.
Others, though, plunder both—and great their prize.

On St Urban's day (25 May) assaults are mounted by the French in the area of Tarsus and Antakya (ancient Antioch), near the Turkish border with Syria, while other allied forces come ashore further north, around Istanbul. And as a result the whole of the Levant—Jerusalem included—is soon freed from the oppressive yoke of the occupiers (II.22, VI.85).

As ever, there are of course some standing on the sidelines who are canny enough to profit from the conflict (see VIII.83 above). Little good does it do the beleaguered Israelis, though, whose country is now in utter ruins (*Sixain* 34), much as the

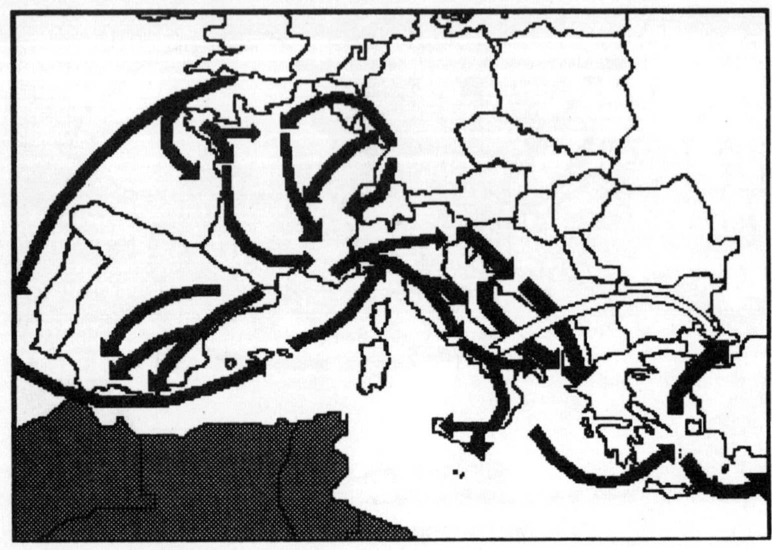

The Western counter-invasion: final summary chart

Bible's various apocalyptic doom-scenarios themselves anticipate:

> *Princes and lords make war upon each other,*
> *Cousin 'gainst cousin, brother against his brother—*
> *Till Bourbon makes an end of Araby.*
> *The friendly rulers of Jerusalem*
> *Shall by the awful crimes performed on them*
> *To ruin be condemned and penury.*

Nevertheless, extreme measures still have to be applied before final victory can be won. At *Century* II.70 there are even signs of a devastating Western nuclear attack. As a result, the enemy high command is forced to retreat from Istanbul to Trabzon (the former Trebizond), while in the newly liberated lands around the Mediterranean there is a surprising willingness by former Muslims to adopt the incomers' Christianity (IX.43, VII.36).

A new Messiah?

The Christian Henri, evidently, has made an extraordinary impression on friend and foe alike. By St Matthew's Day (21 September) he is universally regarded as the great liberator and saviour (II.79, VI.70). *Présage* 38 sums up his triumph:

Acclaimed as Victor-Emperor is the King;
To tainted Church the royal deed proclaimed.
On Matthew's day they shall his triumph sing
O'er haughty race, repentant now and tamed.

Is he, then, some sort of Messiah? Certainly **Nostradamus** strongly suggests the possibility (V.52, V.79):

A king there'll be who'll turn things upside down,
Placing poor refugees in high esteem.
The pure and chaste, once used in blood to drown,
Long time shall flourish under such regime.

All sacred pomp its wings shall soon abase
Once the Great Legislator starts his reign.
He'll raise the lowly, far the rebels chase.
None like him shall be born on earth again.

The phrase 'on earth', as we shall see, may well be important.

Henri it is who now takes on responsibility for re-establishing civilised institutions throughout the liberated lands, for setting up war-trials, reviving long-abandoned transport-systems, reburying the bodies of France's dead exiles and reallocating land and property whose owners and titles have long since disappeared (IX.66, II.95, IV.20, II.19).

Perhaps above all, though, Henri sees it as his task to re-establish Christianity on entirely new bases. Or rather on very old bases—for the new religion of the West turns out (as we have already anticipated, and **Jeane Dixon** confirms) to owe much more to Christianity's original teachings and to the practices of the early Church than to the enormous, top-heavy edifices of established religion with which we are more familiar today.

As *Century* II.8 puts it:

Of churches hallowed in old Roman manner
They shall reject the very fundaments,
Making base-principles their human banner
At many a former saintly cult's expense.

And so the world is rebuilt anew, and a virtual Golden Age ensues (X.89):

In marble shall they brick walls reconstruct:
Of peace seven years and fifty shall there be.
For humans joy; rebuilt each aqueduct;
Health, honeyed times and rich fecundity.

It is an astonishing transformation, and one for which Henri seems to be held personally responsible, almost as if he were indeed some kind of Messiah. Moreover, within a couple of years the **Great Pyramid**, too, seems to be forecasting the arrival of the first of four Messianic figures via the portcullis-symbolism of its extraordinary so-called Antechamber. The particular portcullis involved, though (the far left-hand one in the diagram overleaf, apparently indicating some kind of 'irruption from above') does not reach the ground: it seems, in other words, to speak more of a semi-Messiah than of a full-blooded one. It is as though whoever is involved—proclaimed as early as 2034, and theoretically destined to preside over the world from 2039 to 2116—is a figure in whom the Divine power is as yet only partially incarnated. Only later, as the three further portcullises reveal, will more inspired and powerful figures appear, destined to transform human life utterly all the way down to ground level. And these, as **Mario de Sabato** reveals, are quite likely to

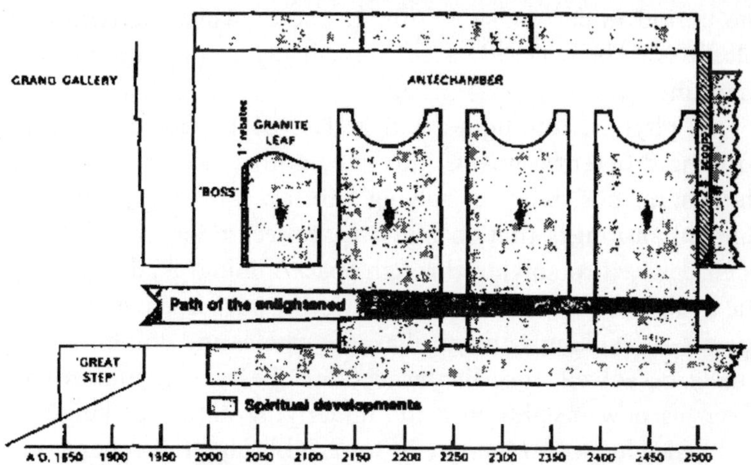

Messianic symbolism in the portcullises of the Great Pyramid's Antechamber[11] (compare the reversed general diagram on page 10)

be not heavenly beings in the religious sense at all, but physical extraterrestrials from a planet whose civilisation is many centuries in advance of ours . . .

Perhaps it is no accident, then, that Henri cannot possibly be the promised Messiah expected by the Jewish scriptures. For the latter has inevitably to fulfil certain very strict conditions. He must, for a start, be born a Jew in the town of Bethlehem, and he must also be recognisable as the ancient King David returned. Possibly, indeed, that must actually be his name.

Nevertheless, it is with a so-called 'boss' *in the shape of the Egyptian hieroglyph for 'bread'* that the 'suspended' portcullis that seems to represent him in the **Great Pyramid** turns out to be marked. It is also apparently 'broken off from above'. The presumably deliberate symbolism is apt—for some there will certainly be who will regard his advent, in true Messianic tradition, as nothing less than manna from heaven.

Humanity comes back down to earth

And, curiously enough, coming down to earth from heaven looks likely to become very much the theme of the moment. For the period under consideration is one in which, if **Arthur C. Clarke** is to be believed, scientists will strike gold in more ways than one.

In physics, techniques will at last be perfected for transforming different elements into one another, so actually raising the distant possibility of solving here on earth the problem of mineral shortages that so much space-technology has hitherto been devoted to solving through space-mining. And in biology the problem of communicating with the more intelligent animal species—the chimps and gorillas, the whales and dolphins—will finally be solved, too. But not before the related studies have given us new insights into the underlying nature of language, and hence helped to prepare us for establishing full contact with our new-found extraterrestrial friends.

In both areas, then, our studies will unwittingly have prepared us for the coming Great Encounter. It is our search for minerals that will have helped us to make contact in the first place. And it is our quest for communication that will have helped prepare us to seal that contact in a true interchange of knowledge.

Earth and heaven, in short, will have fructified each other. And that, it seems—truly ancient though the notion is—is likely increasingly to become the theme of the future, too.

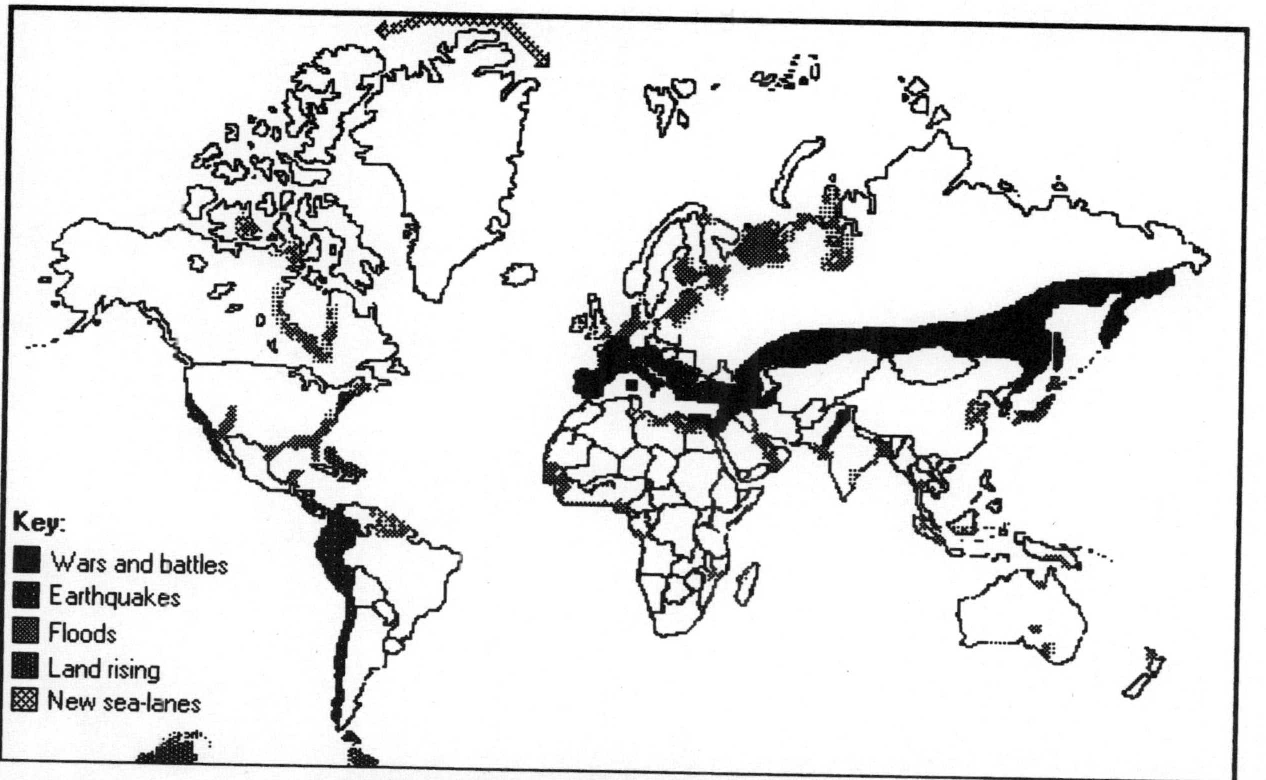

Possible world-upheavals in the twenty-first century

Part Three

Calendar for Generations to Come

THE LONGER VIEW

So far we have been taking a detailed look at the years that people now alive might hope to see. Now the time has come to go further and survey, first of all, the times of their children and grandchildren, and then the long vistas of centuries to come.

For such centuries, it seems, there will surely be.

As the distance grows between those times and this, perspective inevitably comes into play. Events that—from where we now stand—seem close together, start, in reality, to get further and further apart.

And so the seers' vision puts on seven-league boots, as it marches with ever-lengthening strides into the far reaches of the future . . .

2041-2100

• Date Summary •

Arrows indicate the beginning ↓ and end ↑ of a prophetic window

2041		
	2044↑	Last likely date for final defeat of Asiatic empire and beginning of era of unparalleled peace and prosperity (*Nostradamus*)
2050	↕	Many lower-lying parts of the world overwhelmed by rising sea-levels (*John Gribbin et al.*)
	↕	Gravity control and suspended animation achieved (*Arthur C. Clarke*)
	2052	Rapid material recovery experienced world-wide (*Great Pyramid*)
	↕	Human memory playback developed (*Arthur C. Clarke*)
	↕	A new space-drive developed, leading to deep space exploration and terraforming of inhospitable planets (*Arthur C. Clarke*)

2060	↕	Space-time warping achieved (*Arthur C. Clarke*)
	2062	Final collapse of Asiatic empire in the East (*Nostradamus*)
	↕	Artificial life created (*Arthur C. Clarke*)
2070	↕	Control of earth's climate starts to be achieved (*Arthur C. Clarke*)
	2072↓	Beginning of era of enormous physical prosperity and achievement (*Great Pyramid*)
	2073↓	Beginning of era of massive spiritual expansion, with humanity raised to new levels (*Great Pyramid*)
	↕	Near-light speeds reached (*Arthur C. Clarke*)
2080	↕	Artificial intelligence starts to exceed man's (*Arthur C. Clarke*)
	↕	First interstellar flights undertaken (*Arthur C. Clarke*)
2090	↕	Teleportation and matter-replicators developed (*Arthur C. Clarke*)
	↕	First actual meetings with extraterrestrials (*Arthur C. Clarke*)
	↕	World-linkage of human consciousness finally achieved, leading to effective immortality (*Arthur C. Clarke*)

2100	↕	Approximate end of initial era of world peace and prosperity (Nostradamus)
	↕	Stellar engineering begins (*Arthur C. Clarke*)

•COMMENTARY•

BY THE MIDDLE OF THE TWENTY-FIRST CENTURY THE SEA-LEVEL RISES long predicted by present-day climatologists[6] may well be starting to wreak devastation world-wide, failing the building of sea-defences of an improbable magnitude. In many ways the resulting situation is strongly reminiscent of **Edgar Cayce**'s predictions for the beginning of the century.

In the United States, large swathes of South Carolina, Florida and coastal Louisiana and Texas are set to go underwater. Further north, the cities of New York, Atlantic City and Boston will all be flooded. Elsewhere in the world, Bangladesh and the Maldives will be overwhelmed, as will Venice, the northern part of the Nile Delta (including the city of Alexandria) and much of the Low Countries. In Britain, most of Norfolk and the land around the Thames Estuary will be lost.

The world, in short, will be an increasingly watery one—though at the very same time the southern deserts of the northern hemisphere will be steadily marching north.

The silver lining

As ever, though, there is a positive side to it all. If the deserts are marching north, then so is the temperate zone. Consequently ever vaster tracts of previously uncultivable heath and even tundra will for the first time come under serious cultivation, while northern Europe will be enjoying a positively Mediterranean climate. Winter as we have known it will, as **Mario de Sabato** has long anticipated, be abolished.

The world's food supply, consequently, should actually increase rather than decrease.

Perhaps it is not too surprising, then, that most of the rest of the predictions for this period are remarkably positive in tone. Indeed, what is possibly most astonishing about them is the way in which they all seem to dovetail with one another. The **Great Pyramid** and **Arthur C. Clarke**, in particular, both seem to foresee the most extraordinary developments for the second half of the twenty-first century, all of them redolent of just such an era of peace and massive scientific and social progress as **Nostradamus** predicts.

True, there is something distinctly science-fictional about many of the developments listed by **Arthur C. Clarke.** From a serious science-fiction writer we should expect nothing less. And yet the visions of the great science-fictionists—and of **Clarke** in particular—have an astonishing way of turning into actual, physical realities. Such writers are, in a sense, our modern prophets, weaving out of the stuff of their fertile imaginations a carpet upon which the rest of us are subsequently seduced into walking, totally unaware for the most part that what we take for earth-stuff is really only mind-stuff.

As **Nostradamus** puts it at *Century* VI.61, apparently aware that his own homeland may be the last fully to appreciate the gist of his prophecies (no doubt because future generations would be baffled by his arcane and, to them, old-fashioned French):

> *Scarce yet unrolled, the mighty tapestry*
> *As yet but half of history makes known:*
> *Driv'n far from France, cruel it shall seem to be*
> *Till all in face of war its truth shall own.*

Carpets and tapestries woven out of our own mind-stuff, in fact, have a remarkable habit of turning into realities. And possibly this is because they *are* realities.

The reason is quite simple. Although we may *assume* that we observe the world directly and dispassionately, in fact (as any conjuror can demonstrate and any optical illusion prove) we see it only as we think it is. To a large extent our brain actually creates a world of its own devising out of our incoming sense-impressions, and whether the two really correspond is something that we can never hope to find out. The result is that what we actually experience is not the world that is 'out there', but our *perceptions* of the world that is 'out there'—which is no doubt why our own inner conflicts (as the great psychologist C. G. Jung realised) so often seem to come back at us from 'out there' with such extraordinarily overwhelming force.

It is almost as though we are living in a dream-world from which we are unable to escape. Made of mere dream-stuff though it may be, to us who are imprisoned within the dream it seems every bit as hard as iron.

This takes us back, then, to the point that I made at the very beginning. The future that we shall all experience is actually a future that we ourselves have created, not merely by our actions, but also by our very thoughts and expectations, our subconscious fears and hatreds, our unresolved inner problems.

So that we shall actually get the future that we deserve.

In effect, then, the universe presents us with the perfect feedback-system. Whatever we do 'in here' is subsequently reflected 'out there'. Indeed, between the 'in here' and the 'out there' there is ultimately no practical difference, since the only place in which we can ever experience either is 'in here'.

And so the world turns out to be our very exercise-book, the cosmos our classroom. We are in the ultimate learning-environment. We can learn our lessons the easy way, or we can learn them the hard way. Paradoxical as it may seem, learning them the easy way involves actually making some effort to take them on board, while learning them the hard way means doing little or nothing to start with, only to find afterwards that ultimately it hurts a lot more.

'Lazy people,' as the unforgiving saying has it, 'always take the most pains.'

Thus it is that human consciousness will continue to develop and evolve whether we like it or not. As mobile animals, the very law of our existence demands that we move from here to there. And though 'here' may seem a more comfortable place to be, 'there' is where we ultimately belong—even if, once we get 'there', we discover that it in turn has unaccountably become 'here'.

And that, in the first instance, means getting off our backsides.

Our future curriculum

The events already foreshadowed in this book show this process in action. Unable or unwilling to take sufficient steps to remove from our world the prejudices and injustices, the hatreds and exploitations that we in the rich West are only too keen to enjoy as long as they are to our own advantage and we do not notice them, we shall find the world on to which we are projecting all these monstrosities beating its way to our doorstep and depositing them all back on our own doormat. Having kicked the Third World in the teeth for far too long—and the Muslim world in particular—we shall suddenly find ourselves, too, in need of emergency dentistry as Europe succumbs to the invaders.

Or do we really think that we can continue to get away almost literally with murder?

The painful lessons once learnt, however, all sorts of possibilities start to open up for us. Not merely do our own teeth start to hurt a lot less (largely because most of them have, willy nilly, been removed), but our whole life starts to improve by leaps and bounds. Our living conditions, our social interactions, our science and technology, even our very consciousness are lifted on to entirely new levels. Starting by transforming our own planet once more into the Garden of Eden that in reality it always was, we shall go on to transform other planets, too—even to engineer whole star-systems, if **Arthur C. Clarke** is to be believed. Having succeeded in linking our individual consciousnesses together into a single super-consciousness—perhaps with the aid of the machines that will by then be starting to become even more intelligent (and hopefully less potentially stupid) than ourselves—we shall find that almost nothing is impossible. In particular (as **Jeane Dixon, Mario de Sabato** and **Arthur C. Clarke** all predict), suddenly we shall find that we can cross the cosmos as easily as we now cross the seas. In the process we shall finally meet those long-sought, super-advanced aliens with whom we have been communicating for so long, and perhaps in future learn to benefit from the knowledge and deeper insights that they, too, have acquired—no doubt at the cost of much pain of their own.

But let us not imagine that we can then treat them as we once treated our poorer neighbours here on earth. Our newly acquired holistic form of consciousness should admittedly help to prevent this. But if it fails to do so, of one thing we can be sure.

The painful lessons, as **Nostradamus** hints, will have to begin all over again.

2101-2500

• DATE SUMMARY •

Arrows indicate the beginning ↓ and end ↑ of a prophetic window

2101 ↓		New York being rebuilt after earlier destruction; industry dispersed; houses made of glass; Nebraska now on new American *west* coast (*Edgar Cayce*)
	2116	Death of first semi-Messianic figure (*Great Pyramid*)
	2129↕	Path of spiritual evolution closed to still-unenlightened humanity (*Great Pyramid*)
	2134	Second, more powerful Messianic figure arrives (*Great Pyramid*)
	2163↓	Arrival on earth of being from another, much more advanced planet, destined to transform human civilisation (*Mario de Sabato*)
	↓	New world order established, bringing universal peace and prosperity (*Mario de Sabato*)

2101	2163↓	Beginning of 'Prophetic' phase of the Golden Age, during which the shape of the entire future will be determined (*Mario de Sabato*)
	↓	New propulsion techniques make space travel as easy as modern air-travel (*Mario de Sabato*)
	2191↑	Last likely date for visitation of being from other planet, leading to arrival of other extraterrestrial visitors like the first (*Mario de Sabato*)
2200		
	2238	Second Messianic figure dies or departs (*Great Pyramid*)
	2264	Third Messianic figure appears (*Great Pyramid*)
	2279↓	Beginning of initiatory or reintegrative period for idealistic or religious-minded people (*Great Pyramid*)
2300		
	2368	Third Messianic figure dies or departs (*Great Pyramid*)
	2375↕	Astrological start of Age of Aquarius (*Aeonic astrology*)
	2394	Fourth Messianic figure appears (*Great Pyramid*)
2400		
	2422↓	Attempted last-minute reform among still-unenlightened humanity (*Great Pyramid*)

2400		
	2477↑	End of last-minute reform-attempt among still-unenlightened humanity (*Great Pyramid*)
	2499	Humanity's window for transformation to higher levels of consciousness and existence finally closes: period of intense preparation begins (*Great Pyramid*)
2500		

•COMMENTARY•

FROM THIS POINT ON WE ARE INTO A PERIOD OF STRANGE, ALMOST incomprehensible developments involving the very transformation of human consciousness itself. Inevitably they are extremely difficult to talk about. Two caterpillars might as well attempt to discuss how butterflies manage to fly when neither really believes in them in the first place.

Nevertheless both the **Great Pyramid** and the **Bible** offer us some familiar clues, while **Mario de Sabato** describes what is likely to happen in terms that will at least be familiar to readers of science-fiction. This particular genre, as it happens, not only has a knack of anticipating the future: it also provides us with a suitable vocabulary for discussing it.

And what is involved, it seems, is a whole series of Close Encounters designed to speed up our evolution by several centuries in as many years.

Such a process cannot help but be painful. There will be constant dangers of burn-out. But somehow, behind all the dispassionate listing of events, there seems to be a sense of extraordinary urgency. It is as if there is only a limited time left for us to make the grade before some kind of cosmic winter descends, leaving us 'caterpillars' still unmetamorphosed into the chrysalises—let alone the butterflies—that alone will have any hope of propagating the species.

Indeed, **Edgar Cayce**'s extraordinary revelation for the early years of the twenty-second century suggests that the planetary change may already have begun—for his dramatic prediction for the central state of Nebraska suggests that, following the anticipated polar toppling, east has in some way become west and vice versa. Further fundamental upheavals of some kind or other, then, must surely be in train, however distant their eventual expression.

The great transformation of humanity

The great Close Encounter programme is set to begin at some date between 2134 and 2191—and in the most astonishing of ways, at that. **Mario de Sabato** can scarcely conceal his excitement. Somewhere in the area of Palestine, he says, an almost god-like extraterrestrial being, apparently of white human race and speaking a language curiously akin to Hebrew, will suddenly appear and be welcomed by Jews and Christians alike as the promised Messiah. In fact, though, he will have come not from 'heaven' in the biblical sense but from another, much more advanced planet whose acquired knowledge and wisdom he will then proceed to share with us—and, as a result, human evolution will be advanced by several centuries in as many years. At the same time ageing will be postponed, the human lifespan extended and the whole question of reincarnation and the afterlife finally settled.

Whether the lordly visitor is 'really' the Messiah or 'really' a mere extraterrestrial will of course be neither here nor there. The future Messiah—in his Christian form, at least—was always expected to be an extraterrestrial *by definition*: in other words, he was always expected to come from heaven (i.e. the sky) and to descend amidst the clouds. Perhaps that is why the visitor's distant sponsors, having possibly studied us for centuries and long anticipated the risk of rejection as 'aliens', seem set to take so much care to fulfil the ancient Messianic expectations in almost every detail.

Yet what we choose to call him or how we care to define him are of little consequence. What matters is less who he is than what he actually does.

And in the event he turns out almost literally to be our salvation.

Moreover, he will not by any means be the last of his kind. News as it may be to present-day Jews, Christians and Muslims, both the **Great Pyramid** and **Mario de Sabato** reveal that there are to be further visitors from 'out there' (see pp. 175–6), all of them contributing in turn to our ultimate transformation into 'gods' in our own right (as seen from the point of view of our present-day knowledge and technology, that is).

In short, the visitors will act as a kind of collective cosmic midwife, their self-imposed task to usher us safely into the new world of the Age of Aquarius, rather like the race dubbed 'the Overlords' in **Arthur C. Clarke**'s intriguing novel *Childhood's End*. And we, for our part, will need by then to have developed our communal consciousness to the point where the risk of neurological overload and consequent burn-out is minimised. There is, after all, a limit to how much new information we can hope to absorb and process at any one time. Here I am reminded of Fred Hoyle's equally intriguing novel *The Black Cloud*, in which just such a burn-out is described—a fact which once again demonstrates how valuable a service our great science-fictionists have done us by anticipating such events in advance, however imperfectly.

However, there will presumably be some who are unwilling to participate in such developments at all—whether because they simply cannot be bothered, because they are blinded by planetary xenophobia, or because their religions or inherited belief-systems simply do not allow them to. The **Great Pyramid** seems to anticipate particularly severe problems here for the materially-minded and the religiously-minded alike, stuck as both tend to be in rigid, inherited systems of thought. Such people there will of course always be. And for this reason some kind of divide must eventually occur between those who are prepared to move with the times and those who are not. Not because it is imposed by anyone, but because that is what people themselves will choose. This too, indeed, seems to be reflected in the **Great Pyramid's** revelations for the latter end of the current period.

But what practical effects it will have is something for even later predictions to reveal . . .

2501-4500

• Date Summary •

Arrows indicate the beginning ↓ and end ↑ of a prophetic window

2501		
	2533↓	Start of 'Apocalyptic' phase of Golden Age (*Mario de Sabato*)
	↓	Sky turns bright orange: clouds no longer appear (*Mario de Sabato*)
	↓	Separate areas of the earth set apart for different lifestyles and proclivities (*Mario de Sabato*)
	2561↑	Last likely date for all the above (*Mario de Sabato*)
	2569	End of totally materialistic, unenlightened forms of civilisation (*Great Pyramid*)
2600		

2700		
	2737↕	End of 'Apocalyptic' phase of Golden Age: 'unenlightened' areas of earth destroyed by natural forces (*Mario de Sabato*)
2800	↕	Beginning of New Era for entire universe, including planet earth (*Mario de Sabato*)
	2828	End of present age: beginning of true Millennium (*Nostradamus*)
2900		
	2989	Beginning of Millennium, or Golden Age on earth, for fully enlightened, reintegrated humanity (*Great Pyramid*)
3000		
	3279	Possible end of initiatory era for conventionally religious humanity (*Great Pyramid*)
	3797	End of earthly Millennium: new, temporary period of growing troubles leading up to final Kingdom of Heaven (*Nostradamus*)
	3989	End of earthly Millennium for fully enlightened, reintegrated humanity: entry into higher dimensions of being and/or consciousness entirely (*Great Pyramid*)
4000		
	4500↕	End of Age of Aquarius and beginning of Age of Capricorn (*Aeonic astrology*)

•COMMENTARY•

ONCE AGAIN IT IS EXTREMELY DIFFICULT TO SAY ANYTHING DEFInite about what these ultimate events for humanity really mean. Clearly vast changes are afoot, and it at last starts to become clear why the initiatives already described were so urgent. Evidently some kind of disaster—or even a whole series of them—is due to overwhelm the earth, and only those prepared for it are likely to be able to survive to repropagate the species in the aftermath. Indeed, **Mario de Sabato** suggests specifically that the catastrophe will spare only those few regions of the earth where true wisdom has come to reign.

The catastrophe, he predicts, will be natural in origin, though linked to the lurking residue of former human nuclear experiments. **Nostradamus,** too, seems to expect something similar, writing of 'hidden fires' that will lay waste huge tracts of countryside—to say nothing of droughts and searing winds (*Century* IV.67). Perhaps as a result, growing food shortages and consequent inflation will loom world-wide, both heralded by an 'unwonted bird' that is clearly none other than the celebrated premonitory eagle of St John's Revelation (*Centuries* I.67, II.75). 'Huy! Huy!' it cries in the seer's covering letter to King Henri II, so echoing the biblical eagle's 'Oee! Oee!' (Alas! Alas!). *But perhaps it is significant that, in Old French, the word* 'huy' *meant 'today'.*

So severe is the famine and so unprecedented the consequent inflation that, according to **Nostradamus,** people will start to grub up roots for food, and even turn to cannibalism.

But then the seer also anticipates some kind of interplanetary collision at around this time (seemingly with a comet), resulting in huge clouds of dust or smoke that will obscure both sun and moon for years on end. The alien celestial body will, he suggests, first appear in the heavens like the seventh stone from St John's Revelation—a golden-yellow precious stone called chrysolite—just at the moment when everybody is congratulating each other on how fortunate and successful they are (V.32). Possibly, then, it is the great collision that is really to blame for the fire-storms and searing winds—and so for the consequent food shortages—as well as signalling the end of the age (II.46). For in its wake there will, he warns, be plagues, wars, famines and droughts, followed by a long period of intense cold (III.4).

It is at this point (seemingly on the very cusp of March and April) that **Nostradamus** seems to refer to the expected extraterrestrial saviours (III.5) that are also described by **Mario de Sabato,** even though there seems to be some kind of terrible accident, or even initial military resistance (*Century* II.45):

Too much high heaven the Androgyne bewails,
New-born aloft the sky where blood is sprayed.
Too late that death a mighty race avails.
Sooner or later comes the hoped-for aid.

At *Century* I.91, consequently, the human race is warned by the 'gods' that it, and it alone, must take responsibility for the ensuing conflict. However, the warning goes unheeded, and hostilities merely intensify, even amid the gloom of the growing planetary catastrophe.

In fact, the weather remains disturbed for at least forty years (I.17), and during the continuing earthly conflicts the extraterrestrial visitors wisely choose to stay aloof, orbiting at approximately the altitude of the former American Skylab. The verse in question (VI.5) is an extraordinary one, apparently using the word *Samarobryn* to refer (in the plural) to a whole fleet of space-ships or space-stations. Even more extraordinarily, the term seems to be made up of linguistic elements that, in Russian, mean 'self-operating' or even 'self-sufficient':[13]

A wave of plague shall bring so great a dearth
While ceaseless rains the Arctic Pole shall sweep:
Samarobryn, a hundred leagues from earth,
Law-free themselves from politics shall keep.

Thus it is that amid huge upheavals and conflicts the Old Age moves towards its close for those who are still subject to it, while for those who have successfully survived their course in speeded-up evolution a New Era of unlimited possibilities dawns, however conventionally religious the language in which **Nostradamus** chooses to describe it (II.13, III.2):

The soulless corpse shall never suffer more:
The day of death leads on to birth anew.
The Holy Ghost its rapture shall restore
As soul th' eternal Word shall plainly view.

The Word Divine shall grant to substance crude
All heaven and earth, all mystic gold occult.
To body, spirit, soul all power accrued
O'er earth and heaven—such is the great result.

That New Era is, of course, none other than the dawning Age of Capricorn the Cosmic Goat (originally the Goat-*Fish*), as well as of his 'ruler' Saturn—who is, of course, not merely Old Father Time, but the Grim Reaper himself. '*Stretch forth your sickle and reap*', calls the angel of St John's Revelation to the coming Son of Man at the time of the End, '*for the reaping-time has come, and earth's harvest is more than ripe.*'

The world that remains, consequently—and certainly the earth *will* remain—is a world not of rich, green crops, but of autumn stubble-lands. Capricorn's is essentially a world of remnants, of picking and gleaning from among what is left, of collecting up the pieces once again and attempting to make something of them. Goats, it is worth remembering, are omnivorous creatures, largely because they have to be.

But if the Goats remain, the more fastidious Sheep, heirs to the former dispensation of Aries, have in some strange way been culled and removed, just as the Jesus of Matthew 25 explicitly anticipates. For them, it seems, the story of humanity is complete. Or rather, the humanity that goes on to inherit a new universe entirely—'a new heaven and new earth', as the **Bible** puts it—will be one that we today would not even recognise.

This is no cause for despair, of course. For it means that our own generation will successfully have completed its task, acting as a truly vital link in the long chain that leads from our primitive forebears to the very summit of earthly evolution.

Part Four

Epilogue

Could It All Come True?

THE HUMAN RACE'S PROSPECTS, CLEARLY, ARE BOTH FEARFUL AND awesome—at least if the prophets are right. But are they right, and how can we possibly know?

Perhaps the first thing to say is that we cannot. We can compare the prophets with each other. We can assess their success-rates in the past. Yet in neither case does this give us any cast-iron guarantees about their success-rates in the future.

We are left—as ultimately we have to be left wherever human perception is concerned—with uncertainty. Quite how unsettling we find that uncertainty will depend very largely on just how certain we think the universe *ought* to be. And here the conclusions of our most advanced philosophers and scientists are in agreement: the answer is 'Not a lot'.

What does seem to be certain, however, is that the future effectively lies in our own hands.

For if, as I suggested at the very beginning, the future is the direct result of our present thoughts and actions, then we actually have control over it. The self-same human consciousness that causes future events can *un*cause them, too. All that is necessary is that we change our consciousness.

Changing our consciousness

This is of course easy to say, but much harder to do, and we may or may not be willing to attempt it. Most of us—and not only the missionaries among us—are much keener to impose it on others than actually to undertake it ourselves.

For it is bound to involve taking some unpleasant and even painful measures. One of them is careful, dispassionate thinking—a thinking so profound as to risk undermining the very foundations of thought itself. And this has, of course, to include an examination of the very bases of our sense-impressions, our perceptions, our assumptions, our likes and dislikes—in short, of our very existence.

This might profitably start with the question, 'Who am I?', and might then go on to ask the supplementary question, 'Yes, but who am *I*—the "I" who am currently being aware of that "I"?' Or is the awareness all?

This process, rigorously pursued, is likely to lead to the eventual realisation that the world we experience is largely one that we ourselves have constructed inside our own heads, and that for all our pretended knowledge of the world 'out there', we can never actually progress any further forward than the backs of our own eyeballs. And the upshot of all this is likely to be that we shall finally have to accept the total relativity of all our human experience.[9]

The final answers that we have been looking for, in other words—indeed, that some of us think they have already found—simply do not exist. There are only questions.

Nothing is certain. Nothing is fixed. And especially not our future.

But all this is distinctly uncomfortable. It makes us feel insecure. And understandably so, for now we can no longer be sure of anything, not even ourselves. We are denied all our former comfortable delusions. Yet it is precisely this state of *appropriate uncertainty* that we have to get used to if our race is to have any posterity.

It is people who think they have the answers who fail to ask the questions. It is people who are sure about everything who, in the end, demolish everybody else's security. It is people who are determined to improve the world by foisting their own certainties upon it who are most likely to finish up by destroying it.

We have to learn, then, to accept the world as it is and ourselves as we are—warts and all. We have to give up our obsessive quest to divide the universe up into good and evil, into what we accept and what we reject, into 'is' and 'ought to be', into 'us' and 'them'—for otherwise we shall have only a divided world, a kingdom at war with itself. Indeed, ultimately we do not have to construct such dubious approaches to reality in the first place—for the simple reason that we *are* reality.

It is our very insistence on dividing that reality up that also succeeds in giving us the impression that we ourselves are somehow separate from it. The moment we learn to stop doing so, however, the realisation can finally dawn that we and it are one. And once that happens, our potentialities as a species become almost infinite.

We can become truly cosmic beings, the very gods themselves.

The big question

But are we really prepared to undertake that supreme adventure of consciousness? Are we even sufficiently motivated to begin it? Thinking, after all, is something that most people prefer to avoid like the plague. Examining our own motivations, especially, is something that scarcely bears thinking about. The whole thing seems likely to end in pain and tears.

But then, to return to my earlier analogy, so does going to the dentist. Yet most of us realise that it is better to have our teeth seen to in good time—or, even better, to keep them clean and healthy in the first place—than to suffer much worse traumas later on.

Much the same applies to the future of the world. We need to act while there is still time, rather than waiting for some dubious *deus ex machina* who may or may not wave a magic wand for us at the end of it. And this is where the great seers and prophets come in. Much may well depend on just how far we are prepared to heed their warnings and take note of the tell-tale signs.

Even if we fail, however, we should not despair, for the universe will still not be thwarted. It is more than capable of imposing on us events of whatever brutality turn out to be needed to provoke the necessary changes in us. Our own inner conflicts will, as we have seen, be remorselessly reflected 'out there' in the world as we experience it. We shall, if necessary, be dragged kicking and screaming into the next phase of our evolution—quite regardless of whether we like it or not.

So that the over-all process, for all its possible horrors, will still turn out ultimately to be entirely benevolent.

'Spare the rod,' the ancient wisdom proclaimed, 'and spoil the child.' No doubt something of the same dynamic applies to us, too. Yet, as in child-rearing, that does not have to be the way of things. We can, if we choose, go willingly to meet our future.

In which case (rather as those who have experienced near-death experiences so often confirm) we can be fairly confident that equally willing hands will be there to assist us on our way.

The future, in short, is unquestionably there. It will happen. The only doubt is over whether we have the courage and wisdom to grasp it by the hand.

Have we?

Have you?

On the answers, clearly, much will depend.

Reference—Bibliography

1 Berlitz, C., *The Mystery of Atlantis* (Souvenir, 1976)
2 Carter, M. E., *Edgar Cayce on Prophecy* (Paperback Library, New York, 1968)
3 Clarke, A. C., *Profiles of the Future* (Pan, 1973)
4 Dixon, J., *My Life and Prophecies* (Muller, 1971)
5 Glass, J., *The Story of Fulfilled Prophecy* (Cassell, 1969)
6 Gribbin, J., *Hothouse Earth* (Bantam, 1990)
7 Kinsman, F., *Future Tense* (Pendulum, 1980)
8 Lemesurier, P., *The Armageddon Script* (Element, 1981)
9 Lemesurier, P., *Beyond All Belief* (Element, 1983)
10 Lemesurier, P., *Gospel of the Stars* (Element, 1990)
11 Lemesurier, P., *The Great Pyramid Decoded* (Element, 1977)
12 Lemesurier, P., *The Great Pyramid: Your Personal Guide* (Element, 1987)
13 Lemesurier, P., *Nostradamus—The Next 50 Years* (Piatkus, 1993)
14 Lemesurier, P., *This New Age Business* (Findhorn, 1990)
15 Nostradamus, M., *Les Prophéties*, especially in the following editions and works:
du Rosne, A. (1557)
Rigaud, B. (1568)
Reynaud-Plense, C., *Les vraies Centuries et Prophéties de Michel Nostradamus* (Imprimerie Régionale, Salon, 1940)

de Fontbrune, J.-C., *Nostradamus: historien et prophète* (du Rocher, 1980)

Leroy, Dr E., *Nostradamus, ses origines, sa vie, son oeuvre* (Laffitte, 1993)

16 de Sabato, M., *Confidences d'un voyant* (Hachette, 1971)

17 de Sabato, M., *25 ans à vivre?* (Pensée Moderne, 1986)

18 Schonfield, H. J., *The Authentic New Testament* (Dobson)

19 Schonfield, H. J., *The Passover Plot* (Hutchinson, 1965)

20 Tomas, A., *Beyond the Time Barrier* (Sphere, 1974)